A Sketch of the Kafir and Zulu Wars

A Sketch of the Kafir and Zulu Wars

The Experiences of an Officer of the
Somerset Light Infantry in South Africa
1877-79

Henry Hallam Parr

LEONAUR

A Sketch of the Kafir and Zulu Wars
The Experiences of an Officer of the
Somerset Light Infantry in South Africa
1877-79

by Henry Hallam Parr

First published under the title
A Sketch of the Kafir and Zulu Wars

Leonaur is an imprint
of Oakpast Ltd

ISBN: 978-0-85706-266-6(hardcover)
ISBN: 978-0-85706-265-9 (softcover)

http://www.leonaur.com

Publisher's Notes

The opinions of the authors represent a view of events in which he
was a participant related from his own perspective,
as such the text is relevant as an historical document.

The views expressed in this book are not necessarily
those of the publisher.

Contents

Introduction

There is no place more cheerless than Woolwich Docks in winter, on a bitterly cold, drizzly day in November. Add to the weather a knowledge that you are going to the other end of the world, in a small steamer with three or four hundred raw recruits, and that you have taken leave of various people whom you did not want to leave, and who did not (you fondly imagine) want to lose you; that your favourite haunts will know you no more for many months;—given all this, anyone who is not a trifle low-spirited must be a Mark Tapley indeed.

I think we *were* a little depressed; but the steamer was to start at once, and the draft which we were in charge of was the last to be embarked, so there was no time for reflection, and when the men were got on board, it was time for the smart staff-officer superintending the embarkation to wish us goodbye and get on shore. "Well, goodbye, and good luck," said he, jauntily. "Charming little ship, isn't she? First-rate mess; good wine; plenty of ice; and, *I believe*, a cow!"

How often did we repeat to ourselves during the voyage, with many imaginary marks of exclamation, the above speech! The mess was *not* first-rate; the wine was *not* particularly good; there was no ice, and there was no cow. However, this we had not discovered as we grimly, eyed the above-mentioned staff-officer mount his horse and canter away in the direction of his snug quarters.

I fear I am betraying a bitter and an unforgiving temper while I write of the preparations for our comfort on board the transport. But I will speak of the good ship herself, and of her burly skipper, with the utmost respect. Had they not both been the best of their kind these lines had surely never been written.

Three days after leaving Woolwich we were in a furious storm. The skipper said cheerily enough to the two or three ladies on board that it was bad weather, but would probably soon clear; but to the men he only said that we were all right as long as "things stood." We devoutly hoped they would, and as we held on by our eyelids and watched the ill-fated *La Plata,* the telegraph ship, heavily laden and encumbered with deck hamper, we thanked our fate that we were light in the water.

Things *did* stand (though neither we nor anyone else ever saw the poor *La Plata* again after sundown that evening), and three days more found us off Funchal, looking rather knocked about, but safe.

Oh, the weariness of our voyage from Madeira to the Cape! The little steamer was so light that, if there was the least swell, her screw was as much out of the water as in, and we could only potter along at four or five knots an hour. The cooking was worse than indifferent; and, to add to our trials, a malady broke out among the men, and it was discovered the only remedy which we had to grapple with it was very limited in quantity. However, by energetic precautions the plague was stayed, and after thirty weary days we dropped anchor in Table Bay, and gazed up delighted at Table Mountain, and drank in the scented breeze which blew off to us from the land.

There are not many places more beautiful than Table Mountain, with its ever-varying lights and shades, its cloud tablecloth, its pines and silver trees, and its rushing streams; and the beauty of the lower slopes of the mountain, over which the old Dutch block-houses, posted high up, still stand sentry! Yet how few there are who know or think of it as a beautiful mountain!. The prevailing idea regarding it is, that it overlooks Table Bay, and that it has a flat top. Lovely sugar-bushes with flowers of every imaginable shade and colour, and delicate wild flowers and heaths which in England would be treasured in hot-houses, grow in profusion; and then lower down still come picturesque villages nestled in among pine-woods—the cottages with deep, snug porches, lattice windows, and steep-pitched thatched roofs. A little further out into the country, in the direction of the famed Constantia vineyards, the view is also very beautiful in fine weather, which seems to us, after the limited sunshine we are accustomed to, to be perpetual.

The air is heavy with the perfume of water-lilies and wild flowers and orange blossoms. The atmosphere is so clear that the outline of the blue mountains (whose highest peaks are tipped with snow) stands out against the deep blue sky with fascinating distinctness, and forms a most perfect background to the picture of the old white-gabled farmhouses, surrounded by their vineyards and orange groves.

It would be well if those who are forced to fly for their lives from the cold of England could know what a tempting climate, what scenery, and what varied interests await them in this old Dutch colony.

CHAPTER 1

The Kafir Rising

The session of the Cape Parliament of 1877 was a stormy one. There had been a great battle on the question of frontier defence, and for a short time the issue had seemed doubtful, and the fate of the ministry trembled in the balance.

To a bystander it was all very perplexing. Members of the Eastern provinces of the Cape Colony, who lived in the midst of the Kafirs, rose in the House of Assembly to make vehement speeches, prophesying "that a Kafir rising was imminent, that no preparation to meet it had been made by Government, that the frontier police were useless, that our *Fingo* allies were unwilling to fight, and that if they *were* willing to fight they had only *assegais* to fight with, while the Kafirs were well armed; that it was all very well for Western members to sneer, but if they (the Western members) had the lives of *their* wives and children in jeopardy on the frontier instead of comfortably situated five or six hundred miles away, they might, perhaps, look at the question from a different point of view."

Then a Western member, a supporter of the ministry, would rise and say "that really he was ashamed to hear such panic-stricken utterances; that there was no ground at all for supposing the Kafirs had the slightest idea of rising; on the contrary, they were getting more peaceably inclined every day; that many little Kafir children went to school; that there were many thousand rifles on the frontier, that the police force was in a most efficient state, and that he had great pleasure in assuring the House that the great Gaika chief, Sandilli, whenever he was sober, always expressed himself strongly in favour of peace "(some discontented and obstinate member would here murmur that, as the gentleman in question was nearly always drunk, he did not think this particularly good news), "and that, in fact, there was not the slightest danger of any sort or kind."

This was all very confusing. At first we glowed with sympathy with the Eastern members at the thought of their blazing homesteads and murdered wives and children, and then became red-hot with indignation at the cry of "wolf" being kept up in so obstinate and pertinacious a manner.

However, the rights of the case were soon to be made clear to everyone.

The session came to an end, and the members of the House scattered to their different homes—some by rail to snug old Dutch country towns in the west, some by steamer to the coast and border towns of the east, some by the weary ox-wagon to lone farms in the interior; the Governor and ministers started for the Eastern province, and the metropolis of Cape Colony passed into its dull season.

Shortly, however, this dullness was enlivened by sinister rumours from the frontier. There had been, it was said, a fight between *Fingoes* and Kafirs at a beer-drinking. The Kafirs had gone away vowing vengeance, the magistrates were doubtful whether they could keep the peace, the war spirit seemed rising, and affairs seemed of sufficient gravity to demand the presence of the Governor and ministers at King William's Town, the chief town of the Eastern frontier.

Before going further, we must enter into some explanation of what the disturbing elements on the frontier were composed, and of the whereabouts of the country disturbed, or our story, such as it is, will not be intelligible.

It must first be understood that it is only in the eastern part of the Cape Colony that there are native settlements or "locations." In the west there are natives employed as labourers, railway navvies, and so forth, but only to the eastward of the Great Fish River are tribes found in villages, or *kraals*, living on land allotted to them. Here lies, it may be remarked, the reason for the great want of sympathy between the Eastern and Western provinces of Cape Colony. With the bitter memories of the old Kafir wars still vivid in his mind, with the swarming Kafir population surrounding him, the colonist of the Eastern province looks at every matter in the light it stands with reference to the native question; whereas the Western province merchant or farmer (whose only knowledge of native races is drawn from the industrious Malay or the half-caste Dutch Hottentot) can with difficulty be brought to understand that it is a matter of life and death—or, more prosaically speaking, solvency or ruin—to his Eastern brother

12

that a sound native policy and an efficient system of defence should be maintained on the frontier.

Between the Fish River, then, and the Great Kei (the eastern boundary of the Cape Colony), and between the Great Kei and the River Bashee, natives dwell who have until very lately been engaged in fighting for and against British rule. These natives consist of the *Fingoes* and various subdivisions of the great Amaxosa tribe.

More than fifty years ago, when the bloodthirsty Zulu king, Chaka, was devastating Zulu Land, Natal, and tracts of country still more to the west and north-west, a stream of migration set in towards the country now called "the Transkei" and "the Eastern frontier," consisting of Zulus flying from the vengeance or the tyranny of their king. The Amaxosa were not, it appears, particularly glad to receive them. They were themselves beginning to wish for more land, and the influx of population was, to say the least, inconvenient. Eventually the refugees were allowed to settle down in the Amaxosa country, but only as hewers of wood and drawers of water, and they were given the contemptuous name of "*Fingoes*," or "Dogs."

At the end of the first Kafir war, the British released the *Fingoes* from their bondage, gave them tracts of land in various parts of the country, and set English magistrates over them. These people have made great advances towards civilization and prosperity, and are regarded by the different branches of the Amaxosa nation with the most intense jealousy and hatred. They have always been considered "Government people," and have always fought on our side in the Kafir wars.

The Amaxosa are divided into the following tribes, whose names the late war has made pretty familiar to English ears:—

The Galekas, whose country lies between the Kei and the Bashee, and whose chief, Kreli, is regarded as the paramount chief of the Amaxosa nation; and the Gaikas, who are located in different parts of the frontier, chiefly, however, in the King William's Town district, where their chief Sandilli has his "big place."

It must be remembered that the great difference between the Galekas and the Gaikas is, that the Gaikas (although they have not probably realized the fact very clearly) are British subjects, while the Galekas were before the war only under British protection. Besides the Gaikas and Galekas there are also the Tambookies and the Tembus, who are two nearly related tribes, but located, like the Gaikas and Galekas, on different sides of the river Kei. The Tembus, whose location is the

Transkei north of Galeka Land, have fought with us against the Gale-kas; while most of the Tambookies, who are located in the neighbour-hood of Queen's Town, a town lying about one hundred and twenty miles almost ' due north of King William's Town, revolted, and, under the chief Gongutella, created a diversion in favour of the Gaikas.

All these tribes are more or less uncivilized, and in some parts we have, by permitting the chiefs to hold so much power, allowed the Kafirs to remain as wild and as barbarous as before a white man en-tered their country.

The physical characteristics, language, and descent of all the Kafir tribes, from the western-most part of the eastern province of Cape Colony to the easternmost border of Zulu Land, are nearly the same.

They seem to have no religious forms and few beliefs. They have a vague idea of a "Great-great-great-one," but they never pray and hardly ever allude to him: they have a misty notion that their forefa-thers are dwelling in another land, and believe to a certain extent in ghosts and a spirit-world. In their fables or fairytales a being some-thing between Puck and "Rumpelstiltzkin" figures largely, who is very small and mischievous, milks cows, damages cattle, and torments the men and animals who come in his way, playing them all manner of tricks. He has not apparently any definite name, and it is not very clear whether he is believed in or regarded as a myth.

The most active, and indeed almost the only, belief of the Kafirs is in the power of the witchdoctors, who are responsible for most of the evil worked among the tribes. When any untoward event occurs, the witch-doctors profess to find out the man responsible for it, and his life is made a burden to him if in the Cape Colony; if in Zulu Land he undergoes a process called "smelling out;" his goods are as a matter of course forfeited to the Crown, and he is lucky if he escapes with a whole skin. Curiously enough, men who do not own plenty of cattle and substance are hardly ever "smelt out." Before going to war the warriors of a tribe are doctored all round by the principal witch-doctor. With many and intricate forms a charm is either given or marked on each man to render him invulnerable.

The faith of these people in their chiefs and witchdoctors was shown, our readers may remember, by the suicidal acts of the Gaikas and Galekas in the old war. Their chiefs and witchdoctors preached a gospel to the effect that the time had come when the white man was really to be driven into the sea; that if the Kafirs killed every head of cattle that they possessed, when the last beast was slain all the ancient warriors of their tribe would rise from the sea in tens and tens of thousands, and with their assistance they would drive the hated invader from their land. The result was not as they expected; warriors did come out of the sea, but they were white warriors and fought on the side of their enemies, and the Kafirs were put to desperate straits for food for some time to come. But we are digressing from the war of 1877.

The news then that there were likely to be disturbances on the frontier created great excitement in Cape Town, where an extraordinary amount of vagueness exists about frontier affairs.

The number of warriors Kreli could put in the field was multiplied tenfold, and their fighting powers spoken of with dread.

Public opinion seemed to be doubtful whether it would be prudent to protect the Transkei *Fingoes*, Were we strong enough? If we took the side of the *Fingoes*, would not the Gaikas take the part of the Galekas and rise against us? However, we soon heard that British subjects, although only *Fingoes*, were not to be allowed to be at the mercy of any chief in the Transkei, whoever he might be; for news came down that Kreli had been informed that the *Fingoes* were British subjects, and that if his people attacked them the police would act against the Galekas.

However, this warning had had as yet no results, and at Cape Town we anxiously expected the news of the first engagement, or that Kreli had disbanded his army. The morning of the 27th of September was very stormy, and consequently the telegraph lines worked badly and gave in the slowest and most tantalizing manner possible the news of an action in the Transkei two days before, and an order for reinforcements to be sent up to the frontier at once. This action was called afterwards "The Battle of the Guadana."

The Galeka army, in number about four or five thousand, had attacked a mixed force of eighty police and one thousand five hundred *Fingoes* near Ibeka, the principal police post in Galeka Land.

The *Fingoes* fought with indecision, and when the carriage of the gun the police had with them broke down, they gave way and fled, frightening some of the police horses and unsettling some of the lads who had lately joined the police and who were in charge of them. On this the police were obliged to retreat on Ibeka. On the arrival of this news it was very evident that the question of peace or war was now definitely settled, and the mail steamer leaving Table Bay that day received a good many passengers bound for the frontier to see what was to be seen.

There are many uncomfortable positions in which a man may find himself without being in actual danger or positive pain.

The following has its merits. A blazing sky, a blinding dust, the possession of the third of a box-seat of a Cape cart intended to hold two persons, the two other thirds of the said seat being occupied, the left-hand third by a *Hottentot* boy armed with a cudgel and a cowhide, the right-hand third by a *Hottentot* driver who had been pitched out of the mail-cart the day before and half killed. Both "*Totties*" (as they are called at the Cape) being dressed in old corduroys—and old corduroys and old *Hottentots* are very overpowering!

This was not pleasant, yet when I felt inclined to break from concealed irritation into open wrath, the sight of the poor old *Totty* driver patiently urging on his four miserable horses, bandaged up and plastered, one eye entirely concealed, and the blood oozing from a wound in his head, kept me silent.

Six hours of jolting, flogging, and harness-snapping, of dust, sun, and hot wind, had passed before the poor worn-out horses had brought the Cape cart to the hill above Graham's Town, and before the journey from Port Elizabeth (two-thirds of which had been accomplished by rail) was finished. As the descent of the hill was commenced, and as the pretty little town was caught sight of in the hollow below, it became apparent that something unusual was going on by the numbers of led horses and volunteers in semi-uniform who were passing down into the town.

It turned out that volunteers had been called for, and that a committee of the town was busy buying horses' equipment, etc., for the men who had come forward; and all were busily engaged in organizing a contingent for the front

On leaving Graham's Town the next morning it was soon evident that the country was deserted. There was nothing stirring round any of the farmhouses; not a white man was to be seen; the farmers had evidently "trekked."

The road from Graham's Town to King William's Town is historic ground, and the scene of many skirmishes and fights in the old wars; and on this subject the driver of the Cape cart, in the deliberate manner of those of Dutch blood, told many a story. The cart would have caused a good deal of curiosity if it had appeared on the wood pavement of Piccadilly. It was like a cab (not a four-wheeler or a hansom, but the cab which preceded the mail-phaeton, T-cart, and gig), only much larger and with a low seat in front for the driver; the horses were four wiry little hackneys, the harness plain coarse leather.

Four-in-hand English coachmen might look down on the stolid, stout-built man in a broad-brimmed hat and short jacket, sitting under his horses' tails; and I dare say he would not have looked well on the top of one of the well-appointed coaches which start every summer's morning from Hatchett's, but there was no doubt of his being in the right place where he was—and how he made his horses travel! Before sundown they had made nearly sixty-five miles, and showed but little signs of distress, and amply repaid their owner for the trouble and care he took of them at every stage, and for the judicious way he handled them on the road.

There was no breakfast to be had at the usual halting-place at Great Fish River. The man at the wayside inn was just "*trekking*," and his wagon was loaded ready to start, so another hour saw the cart toiling with hungry occupants through the Fish River bush.

It was here that the Kafirs gave us such trouble during the last war, for its dense cover gave them innumerable opportunities to attack and harass the convoys and bodies of troops which had constantly to make use of the road running through it. It was near here, too, that the only real chance of catching the enemy in the open during the war occurred, and it was not thrown away. The 7th Dragoon Guards charged and recharged the enemy, who said that the mounted warriors must be all chiefs, on account of their size and the beauty of their horses.

An empty stomach does not conduce to bright views of things in general, and we could not help thinking that if in the last Kafir war of 1851-52 between fifteen and twenty thousand troops were required in different parts of the colony, we should be rather short of men now, especially as the Kafirs were reported to be far better armed than formerly.

It was not very long before our seven-pounder mountain guns and our Sniders showed how prodigiously the weapons of the day had strengthened our hands.

At midday the half-way house was reached, and the hungry travellers were greeted by an old lady of nearly ninety. "You have not *trekked* then, ma'am?"

"*Trekked*, is it? may God forgive me if iver I trek and run from a pack of cowardly niggers. I and my sons'll stop here, an' shame maybe'll strike the cowards who have *trekked* when they see an ould woman of near ninety standing her ground."

17

After this I could only hope that the volunteers and *burghers* at the front would be animated with a like spirit to this gallant old lady, who kept her word, and she and her sons held their ground and set an example to the country side during the whole time of the disturbance on the frontier. At six in the evening the halting-place for the night was reached, and at eight next morning the cart drove into King William's Town.

It was evident that the gravity of the situation was realized. Every man strong enough to handle a rifle, and who did not already belong to a volunteer corps, joined the *burgher* corps then being raised for the defence of the town, and came up to drill twice a day at the barracks until pronounced efficient in the rudiments of drill and shooting; and the manner in which middle-aged and even old men accustomed evidently to sedentary occupations stuck to their drill until they had obtained their certificate of efficiency, showed how real they considered the danger to be.

The whole town was crowded with all the white people of the neighbouring districts, and it was pitiable to listen to the story of some of the farmers' wives, who could not afford the expense of lodgings and had to live on the outskirts of the town under their wagons— husband and perhaps eldest son gone to join some volunteer corps, and house and land abandoned to the mercy of fortune.

The feeling of nervousness and excitement throughout the districts containing Kafir locations was very great, and was spreading to those comparatively remote from the frontier. The Government endeavoured to induce people who were at a safe distance to remain on their farms, but with little success, for the conviction seemed universal that, though the Kafirs within the colony were as yet quiet, they were only waiting the signal from their chief Sandilli to rise and make common cause with the Galekas; and the press, with very few exceptions, by publishing all manner of rumours, increased to a very great extent the feeling of alarm and insecurity.

At this juncture, luckily for the colony, it had as the Queen's representative a man who was no stranger to perilous times, who twenty years before in another dependency of the empire had been face to face with dangers a hundred-fold greater than those which now menaced the colony of the Cape of Good Hope.

The situation, it must be granted, was not encouraging. The police force, on which the frontier depended, numbered about one thousand two hundred men, who were scattered all over the frontier, it was hardly known where, and it appeared by the few hundreds which could be got together that this force had been organized on a plan not suitable for the material of which it was composed. In the old Cape war, Sir Walter Currie's police were a most valuable and efficient body, numbering a few hundred men. The men were all colonists, hardy, robust, grown men, used to the rifle and the saddle from boyhood— men who could "spoor" a lost ox, day and night, with eyes like a hawk and ears like a hare. These men did not want anybody to put them up to Kafir tricks and Kafir warfare, or to show them how to take care of themselves or their horses on a journey of two or three hundred miles.

After a time, when it was decided that Her Majesty's troops should be gradually withdrawn from the Cape, and that the colony should prepare to undertake its own defence, the authorities then decided to increase largely the police force, and recruits not being available in the colony in sufficient numbers, they had recourse to England for men.

Recruits came forward, but they were of a different stamp and required a different handling. The boy of eighteen, fresh out from a merchant's desk, who could shoot perhaps a little, had belonged to an English volunteer corps, and had ridden with his sister along the sands at a watering-place, would require a careful training before he could come up to the young colonist who had been accustomed to horses and rifle from boyhood, who had been amongst Kafirs all his life, and whose father had probably fought in the old Kafir wars. The idea was that the recruit did not require any special training or instruction on joining, but that he should be taught to "rough" it; and "rough" it certainly did, and to some purpose, as after a patrol of two or three months' duration through Galeka Land some three years ago, the startling number of twenty *per cent,* of the police lads were invalided. The word lad is used advisedly, as those who joined the police generally remaining only three years in the force, the average age of the men was very young.

Beside the police force there was on the frontier a battalion of the line, the 24th, and at Cape Town another battalion, the 88th Connaught Rangers, and a few artillerymen.

There were also various mounted volunteer corps, who were, as it proved, of immense value, being very much the stamp of Sir Walter Currie's police, without, however, one important quality, *viz.* their discipline.

Although the Galekas, under their chief Kreli, were the only avowed enemy at present (numbering, it was supposed, about eight thousand fighting men), the other tribes in and beyond the colony were, it was acknowledged by those who took the most hopeful view of the case, only waiting to see which way the wind was blowing, and a trifling reverse to our arms would probably increase our enemies tenfold.

The only natives who were heart and soul on our side were the *Fingoes*, and these having no chiefs to egg them on to obtain arms, as in the Kafir tribes, were not extensively armed, nor were they considered equal to the Kafirs in fighting qualities.

The force then at the disposal of the authorities was small; but had there been a settled plan of action, a proper chain of responsibility or defined duties for those in command of the colonial forces, and for the native magistrates and residents; could all hands have been piped to quarters as in a properly found vessel on the alarm of fire—the outlook would not have been so bad. This, however, was impossible. The magistrates seemed to have nothing to do with the police or the police with the magistrates, nor had the officer commanding Her Majesty's troops on the frontier direct connection with any civil authority. No one knew whom to look to for authority, assistance, or information, and matters were going on from bad to worse, when luckily Sir Bartle Frere arrived at King William's Town, and, with one of his ministers and the general commanding, began to evolve some sort of order out of the chaos.

Chapter 2

Ibeka

The action of the Guadana, as has been mentioned, was fought on the 24th of September. By the first week in October matters looked considerably brighter: the general commanding had been definitely placed in command of all colonial forces in the colony and Transkei; Mr. Griffith, a gentleman of considerable experience, and one who possessed the confidence of the colonists, had been placed under him, in command of the colonial troops in the Transkei, and had fought on the 29th of September a defensive but successful action with the Galekas.

The Galeka chief, Kreli, had attacked the police station at Ibeka, which was thirty-five miles from the Great Kei River, and about eighty-three miles by main road from King William's Town. Ibeka was the nearest station to Kreli's great place, and was a position of no strength, situated in a country of isolated hills. It lay, however, pretty high, the ground falling away on three sides, and there was fortunately no cover near for the enemy to assemble and make a rush from on the position. At three p.m. on the 29th of September, the Galeka army, armed with muzzle-loaders of all descriptions and *assegais*, in number about seven or eight thousand, advanced in three points against Ibeka with considerable determination, singing their war-cry and shouting defiance. The force they attacked consisted of one hundred and eighty frontier police, with three seven- pounder mountain guns and rockets, and of about two thousand *Fingoes*. The guns did good execution, and the *Fingoes* stood their ground, and at dark the Galekas retired, carrying nearly all their dead with them. Our loss was trifling. This action had its due effect on the other tribes, and Sandilli, the chief of the formidable "fighting Gaikas," as the colonists called them, assured his Resident that he meant, always had meant, and always did mean

21

to "sit still."

In the mean time proper dispositions of Her Majesty's troops had been made to guard the line of communications to the Transkei, and to cover the line of railway and hold the most important roads leading towards the impregnable Amatola Mountains, to which the Gaikas had always resorted in former wars with their cattle when hostilities fairly began.

Part of the 88th had been ordered up from Cape Town, and a body of marines and sailors and two field-pieces were landed from Her Majesty's ship *Active*, Among the sailors were a party of West Coast natives—*Kroomen*, and these were regarded by the natives in King William's Town with the greatest curiosity.

It may be thought by some that Her Majesty's troops were hardly in their proper place while the colonial troops were doing the fighting. Much to their disgust and disappointment the soldiers were kept in the colony, and for many a sound reason. Infantry are entirely un-suited for Kafir warfare, and to endeavour to oblige Kafirs to fight when they don't want to do so, unless you can hem them in, is to weary and exhaust your men to no purpose. It was of the greatest im-portance that there should be a sufficient force to overawe the Kafirs within the colony, and prevent the tribes other than the Galekas from rising. And, besides, the Government of the colony were desirous that the outbreak should be regarded as a mere affair of police, which could be settled without having recourse to the active agency of the regular troops.

The action at Ibeka was fought on the 29th of September, and for some days there was a lull in the operations.

Supplies of all kinds, especially ammunition for the *Fingo* levies, were urgently needed, and much difficulty was experienced in fur-nishing them.

There was no colonial commission, nor even the nucleus of one, and this important department had to be hastily organised; in theory the police were supposed to find their own rations, which system might work in peace time, but for men to disperse in an enemy's country, to refurnish themselves with food when their first supply was exhausted, was obviously ridiculous.

Supplies came up slowly, owing to the length of time ox-waggons took to traverse the eighty-three miles from King William's Town to the *depôt* at Ibeka, and from the frequent mistakes due to carelessness and want of method. For instance: a wagon bound with stores for

Ibeka, but part loaded with tents for a station sixty-six miles from King William's Town, would load up with the teams at the bottom, and the man in charge would either forget all about the tents or have to unload his entire cargo to get at them.

On the 9th of October, however, Commandant Griffith, whose strength was about four hundred and fifty police and one hundred mounted volunteers and a strong body of *Fingoes*, advanced against Kreli's great place, which was about six miles from Ibeka. The Galekas were driven out of this position by the guns and rockets, the *kraals* burnt, a quantity of grain and some horses captured, without any loss and little fighting.

A body of about one hundred and twenty volunteers, however, who were advancing to join Commandant Griffith's column, suddenly fell in with a considerable number of Galekas, who advanced to the attack with spirit, lengthening their front as they approached the white men, so as to threaten one or both flanks. Luckily the shooting of the Galekas was very bad, and the volunteers stood their ground firmly and made excellent practice with their Sniders, and the Galekas slowly drew off. As it was, the Kafirs were in such force that they managed to get very close to our men. About fifty Kafirs were killed and many wounded; our loss being two men severely and two men slightly wounded, one horse killed and three or four wounded.

After these actions, it was felt that there was no longer much danger of Kreli carrying out the plan, rightly or wrongly attributed to him, i.e, of crossing the river Kei and entering the colony and the Gaika location, and then making an attack against the Government forces with the Gaika and Galeka warriors combined. After the actions of the 9th of October it was not quite clear what had become of the Galeka army. There was no means of obtaining good intelligence, as there was no properly organized spy or secret service either in the police or native department. It was said, however, that Kreli and his forces were making towards the River Bashee, and would give battle in this neighbourhood. Commandant Griffith's forces by the middle of October had been increased to about one thousand mounted men, police, and volunteers, and a force of *Fingoes* varying from four to five thousand.

On the 17th of October this force, having received sufficient supplies, advanced farther into Galeka Land, moving first down towards the mouth of the River Kei, in order to drive before them a part of the enemy's forces who might be hiding in the neighbourhood. The movements were not very rapid. There were hardly any roads, so that although the country was as a rule open and undulating, sometimes a broken piece was met with which necessitated the waggons making a long detour.

Though to one accustomed only to regular troops the force might seem rather strange, yet had there been a little more organization and discipline to start with, a better force for native warfare could not be found.

Each morning, shortly after daybreak, preparations were made for a start: horses driven in, oxen collected, tents struck, and waggons loaded, and the *Fingoes* sent off to scour the country. About six o'clock the columns were ready to march. There was a halt for two or three hours at about ten or eleven, and then a halt for the night about four or five.

Every evening a good deal of firing would occur amongst the *Fingoes*, as they marched to their camping-ground, and would create a good deal of curiosity in the mind of any one not used to this peculiarity. These people have a dislike to leaving their charges in more than one day, and no *Fingo* ever went about with his gun unloaded, so there was a great deal of unnecessary expenditure of ammunition amongst our native auxiliaries. If at a safe distance the waste was not felt so deeply; but if any one chanced to be in their vicinity and near enough to observe the vague manner in which they pointed their weapons, and the curious distinctness with which the bullets whistled about, this needless waste appeared something very reprehensible.

The *Fingoes* had faults, but they were invaluable allies. They fought with more decision and self-dependence at every skirmish, and made exceedingly good light troops. During a march they scoured the country to the front and on the flanks, thus saving the white troops much work. At night they bivouacked on two, sometimes three, sides of the camp, and much reduced the danger of a night attack; such an attack by Kafirs is, however, almost unknown, as they have a strong objection to fighting in the dark, though they will travel and steal cattle and horses at night.

The moment the position of the camp was chosen the dismount was ordered, and horses were off-saddled, knee-haltered, and driven off to water, and messengers sent off to guide the waggons to the camping-ground. Horses in South Africa are not picketed or hobbled, but "knee-haltered;" that is, the "*reim*," or piece of bullock's hide, is hitched round one of the horse's fore-legs just above the knee. He can feed or roll, but cannot go very fast if haltered short enough. It is a funny sight, six hundred or seven hundred horses moving off together, all their heads solemnly nodding, being pulled down to their knees as the haltered fore-knee is placed on the ground.

As no food could be got until the waggons arrived, they were anxiously looked for, and every one brightened up when the advanced guard of their escort came in sight. Then soon the cracks of the formidable whips were heard, and the cries of the waggon-drivers urging on their tired spans.

The first quality, it may be remarked, of a good waggon-driver is to be able to swear in Dutch. As French is the language of diplomacy, as Italian is the language of love-making, so is South-African Dutch the language of waggon-driving. No amount of flogging and English abuse seems to affect a tired team. An energetic and stalwart Englishman may flog away and use tolerably vehement language, but the oxen don't care; he does not know their individualities, and they despise him as an ignorant foreigner who does not know their language. The moment the ponderous whip is handed to a meagre little Dutch *Hottentot*, he gives a crack above his head as a prelude; then follows a volley of the most astonishing guttural and evil-sounding words, winding up with the name of the ox, who shivers with affright and plunges into the yoke. "*Blesbòk!*" Whack! "*Ah! Englànd, verdompt Englànd!*" and crack! down comes the heavy lash on the unfortunate "*Englànd.*" (The most worthless ox in the team of a Dutch Boer is generally dubbed "*Englànd*") The whole team is suddenly seized with an intense desire for progress, and the waggon, to the delight of those who are waiting for its contents, rolls into camp.

Cattle are the riches of the Kafirs, and round them is concentrated most of their interests. Cattle and women, and politics in exciting times, are the topics of the Kafirs. They have innumerable names for differently marked , cattle; where we have to say "a white and brown ox, with a black patch over his right eye," they would use one word to describe the animal. The way a Kafir lad manages a large herd of cattle which would require ever so many English drovers and their dogs to handle is astonishing. It is a curious sight, too, to watch a well-trained span of oxen driven up to be inspanned or yoked. They are driven close up to the fore wheels of the waggon, with their heads towards it, by the *forelouper*, or leader (the man who leads the first pair of oxen during the journey, generally a Kafir lad); the waggon-driver calls each ox by name, who slouches forward to have his weary neck put again in the yoke.

Poor brutes! A Neapolitan cab-horse, a Moorish pack-animal, are both to be pitied, but the miseries of a trek ox surpasses theirs: everlasting toil, insufficient food when the grass is poor or dry, the ponderous whip, the blood-sucking tick, the heavy load, and, as a rule, a callous master, combine to make the life of the ox of a South African transport rider (as the owner of transport waggons is called) one of the most uninviting in the world.

While Commandant Griffith and his forces scoured Galeka Land with the Galekas and all their cattle and women retreating before them, affairs were not very comfortable on the frontier. Though the alarm occasioned by the fear of Kreli's invading the colony had subsided, yet the colonists felt very insecure, and none of those who had left their farms thought it safe to return to them.

There were two great lines of opinion on the frontier—the smaller and optimist party, and the larger and pessimist party. The first held "that the disturbances were nearly over; that by recent events it was proved that the Galekas were nothing wonderful in the fighting way; that if the Gaikas had been going to rise they would have taken advantage of the opportunity when the Galekas first broke out; that the Kafirs wanted to be quiet and plant their crops, but the farmers leaving their farms, and the false reports and rumours which got about, were almost frightening the Kafirs into rising. There had been, it must be owned, a good many stock thefts, but these occurred because of the drought, which prevented the natives from ploughing, and because some of them were really starving."

To this the pessimist party, among which, by the way, were almost all the older and more experienced colonists, replied that "the Galekas were not yet beaten, but were flying across the Bashee to save their cattle and leave their women and children, as they had done in the last war, and that they would return to fight unencumbered. That then the Gaikas would rise; that, perhaps, some of the Kafirs did wish for peace, but there was a strong war party among the young men, and Sandilli was treacherous, and if he moved for war every man of his tribe would follow him. As for the stock-stealing, it was the ordinary prelude to every Kafir war."

The stock thefts on the frontier were certainly increasing, and, combined with losses from the droughts, were driving the farmers nearly wild. Cases of Gaika Kafirs having turned out armed to prevent stolen oxen being "*spoored*" (tracked) near their *kraals* were reported, and noted as a very bad sign. Business, too, was very much at a stand-still; and, altogether, the year 1877 drew near its close with no very bright prospects for the colony.

Chapter 3

The Burgher Corps

On account of the disturbed state of the frontier, the Government decided to send an officer through the most exposed districts to raise *burgher* corps, organize measures of defence in the towns and villages, and give any assistance that was possible in forming and carrying out projects for resisting attack, in case of a general rising of the Kafirs.

Accordingly, one morning at daybreak, about the middle of December, an officer in undress uniform was to be seen leaving King William's Town, followed by an orderly in the sombre garb of black corduroy, which distinguishes the Mounted Police, leading a spare horse.

It was a pleasant change for the officer (whom we will, for simplicity's sake, call the lieutenant), from a hot and dusty office to the open country, from the chair to the saddle, and he and his companions—biped and quadruped—proceeded in the best temper possible in the direction of the famous Amatola Mountains.

It will be readily understood that preparations for a journey in South Africa are somewhat different from those for European travel.

Dressing-bags with brushes, razors, and scent; boot-boxes, portmanteaus, and hat-boxes, with all sorts of contrivances for keeping shirts without crumpling and hats unruffled, are discovered to be unnecessary.

By hair cut close and a growing beard, brushes and razors are rendered useless. One shirt on and one shirt off, the same allowance of socks and silk handkerchiefs, a loose pair of trousers and shoes, soap, towel, and toothbrush, completes the kit. Let us add—to be really independent—biscuits, sausage, chocolate, and flask.

A man should want nothing more—it being always understood he has waterproof sheet, blanket, canteen, and water-bottle fixed on his saddle, comfortably for himself and his horse. This latter, by the way, also manages to do with very few of the comforts his dandy relations in England require. He is not hard to please; he only stipulates for two or three conditions. If he is expected to do hard work day after day (hard work, be it understood, is from thirty-five and forty to fifty-five and even sixty miles a day), he demands that he be not hurried directly he leaves his stable, with his stomach full of food and water; that his load (he generously leaves its weight to the conscience of his master) is placed firmly and comfortably on his back, and that he is well fed.

These conditions granted, the South African horse waives all luxury; he does not want to have his mane water-brushed and his hoofs oiled before he is mounted, nor any hot water for his legs when he comes in after his long day. He asks that you should walk him the last half-mile of his journey—off-saddle him directly he is arrived at his destination (never mind his back not being cool), let him have a good roll in the most dusty place you can find, a moderate drink of water, and with a sigh of relief he will turn to at his evening meal, enabling you to go indoors in search of yours, with a conviction that you will find him fit to travel at daybreak next morning. Let me here lay stress on the necessity of starting early.

Experience shows that if you make an early start on your day's journey, everything will go well with you; start late, and the misfortunes of a month will crowd themselves into that day. On that day you will lose your road, on that day your saddlery will give way, you will lose your favourite hunting-knife, your horse will fall lame, and you and your companions, human and equine, will arrive at your destinations in a thoroughly unchristian frame of mind.

Our friend the lieutenant, we have said, was in good spirits—he would have been a surly mortal if he had not been on such a lovely morning; the sun appearing above the horizon as a friend and not as a fiery enemy; and though the country around him lay parched and burnt, the beautiful green mountains into whose cool shade he hoped to get the next day, tempted him onwards. Indeed, there was not much near at hand to distract him from watching the night mists clear away from the mountain peaks.

A span of gloomy oxen, debating apparently whether it were better to lie still and rest until their master came to inspan them, or whether the dried-up grass were worth the trouble of rising to eat; a waggon, underneath which the transport drivers were still sleeping rolled up in their blankets; a Kafir boy, dressed in the usual Kafir costume (a curious combination of civilized and savage dress) of old tunic and an apron or kilt of skin and hair, watching some half-starved sheep; some Kafir women from a neighbouring *kraal* wrapped in filthy blankets, their bodies and faces smeared with red clay and carrying firewood on their heads, were the only objects to be seen.

By the afternoon the Lieutenant had arrived at the pretty village of Alice, where he found every man and boy so anxious to be organized into something or other that matters were soon arranged.

Close to Alice is situated the Lovedale Mission station, which the good work of Stewart, Buchanan, and others has made so well known amongst those who take any interest in South Africa and its native question. In truth, there is more done at Lovedale towards spreading civilization amongst the natives than at half the remaining stations in South Africa put together. Lovedale is, in fact, a large industrial school for boys and girls. Religious instruction is combined with instruction in trades, and the specimens of carpentering, waggon-making, book-binding, printing, etc., executed by the natives are not to be despised.

Departing on his way next day, the lieutenant soon found himself among the green Amatolas—a delightful change from the parched and weary lowlands, crying out for rain. Here grateful clouds and mists kept the land green, and great rocks and pleasant breezes kept the traveller and his horse cool.

A *Fingo* policeman beguiled the journey by stories of the scenes which occurred in the neighbourhood during the old wars, and the lieutenant regarded "Pieffer's Kop," "Kafir Kop," "Zwart Kop," and other mountains with increased respect as he journeyed amongst them, listening to their previous history.

By sundown Eland's Post (the "*land*" in "Eland" to be pronounced as in Dutch, like the French "*lande*," or the character of the name is lost) was reached.

Perhaps—though it is hard to believe, so bare is the country of game—elands used, not many years ago, to abound round the old-fashioned village and the little fort of Eland's Post, and on the banks of Eland's River; but now, alas! elands are scarce, and must be sought far away from towns and civilization.

The lieutenant was saddened by thinking on this subject as he approached the village, for it recalled unpleasant memories to him. Some years before, when he and his comrades were about to start for South Africa for the first time, they took to reading with great avidity all the books they could lay hands on about travel and sport in South Africa, and were one and all bitten with a desire to outdo Gordon Gumming, and slay more elephants and lions than any one who had yet been there. Accordingly they invested in an elaborate assortment of guns and rifles, and rendered the life of their colonel and the life of their adjutant wearisome by requesting leave on urgent private affairs, and the hearts of the gunmakers were gladdened by the extensive orders for destructive implements given by these misguided individuals.

Alas! when they arrived at where they expected to find the happy hunting-grounds, where they intended to bowl over a lion before breakfast and an elephant during their afternoon's stroll, they found that in the thirty years which had elapsed between the publication of their books of reference and their arrival, the elephants, lions, hippopotami, elands, and their friends had left the neighbourhood, and had, in the most pusillanimous manner, retired some hundreds of miles into the interior of the country.

Now round Eland's Post there is almost entirely a Dutch population, and these Boers had been demanding arms and ammunition from the Government, and, because this request was not at once granted, there was some feeling of irritation in the neighbourhood. The Dutch farmers wanted to be supplied with arms and ammunition on the simple terms of "free, gratis, for nothing," holding that, as they were in danger, the Government was bound to protect them.

The Government view of the case, however, was somewhat different. The Government held that, in the first place, the farmers ought to have bought arms and ammunition for themselves, as their forefathers would have done, and that they ought not to have remained contentedly without means of defence until a war was imminent. It was also thought only fair that the farmers should, if arms were issued to them, consent to be formed into some organization or another, and give some guarantee that the arms should not be made away with, but should be returned to Government when required.

But the Dutch farmers did not wish to give any return for the guns, and were very suspicious of any proposal emanating from Government.

The Civil Commissioner of the district had called a meeting of the farmers for the next day, at which the lieutenant was to state the wishes of the Government; "but I don't think they will ever be got to join a *burgher* corps," said the Civil Commissioner, whose cheery face and good advice had prevented many a scared farmer from deserting his farm. "They have an unconquerable dislike to restraint of any kind, and it is almost impossible to convince them that, if they joined a corps, they could not be ordered away from their own homes; and, though quite loyal, many of the men even hesitate at the prospect of taking the oath of allegiance, saying they have never taken an oath, and that they do not like binding themselves to anything."

Accordingly, next morning the Court House was crammed full of huge, large-jointed, loose-limbed men, with long beards and hair, the latter growing low down on their foreheads, in some cases nearly to the eyebrows, and with stolid and expressionless faces.

When the Civil Commissioner arrived, the list of those men who had applied for arms was called over, and "*Ya*" was answered to such names as "Jacobus Henricus Nell" or "Fredericus Johannes Marx."

When the roll was finished, after some introductory words by the Civil Commissioner, the lieutenant, speaking in English, told his business, the Commissioner translating into Dutch sentence by sentence.

The lieutenant said the Government wished to help the farmers, and would supply them with arms and ammunition, but on certain conditions. The Government did not want them to leave their homes, nor did they want them to become soldiers; they were required to form themselves into a *burgher* corps under officers elected by themselves. They must promise not to take the arms out of the district, and to return them in good order to the Government when ordered; and they must attend a certain number of drills and shooting meetings.

When the lieutenant had done speaking, a huge, wild-looking young man stepped out from amongst the farmers, and said "he wanted to know why all these conditions were required, and why they were wanted to drill. He could ride and shoot with any man, and would fight the Kafirs to the last drop of his blood, but he would *not* be made a soldier of. He and his fathers had always been free, and he wanted to remain so."

The other farmers did not apparently pay much attention to this man, but when a grey-headed man with a hook nose and an excited eye stepped forward, he was evidently regarded as a spokesman.

He spoke at length, and, as he warmed to his subject, with much energy:"We are all glad Government has sent someone to us to settle about the arms," he said; "but the Government terms are hard. Why does the Government think so much of drill? We know the use of arms as well as our fathers before us, and would fight as well as they did. You, *Mynheer*" (turning to the Civil Commissioner), "you know us all; you know we are all true men, and would fight to the death,

32

but we do not want to become soldiers. Our fathers were never made soldiers, nor do we wish to become soldiers. Who knows what would become of us if we once joined a *burgher* corps! We might be sent away from our wives and children, whom we want to defend. Times are hard; we have lost much cattle, and the drought is doing us much damage. We have to work with pick and hoe ourselves, and to drill twice a week is too much. Will not the '*offizeer*' arrange to have a muster once a month? We would all meet and bring our guns, to show that we had got them, and we would have some shooting, but no drill like the soldiers. No! no drill!" and there was a low chorus of "*Ya, ya! dat ist goot!* no drill.*"

The lieutenant then got up again, and told them that "in four or five drills any man who tried could learn the little that was required; that they might have their drills close to them, so as not to take up their time; that they must not think the Government wanted to deceive them, for the Governor and Government wanted to give them as much help as possible, and these regulations had been made for their good. They were not wanted to leave their farms, nor had the Government any power to make them, but they were wanted to stay near their own homes, and to guard them and to fight together for their wives and children."

At this the spokesman said, "*Ya, ya!* to stay near our homes and fight for our wives and children! What the '*offizeer*' says there is good." And all the other Boers murmured, "*Ya! dat ist goot!*"

After a few other questions as to whether the "*offizeer*" could promise that they would not be ordered away from their homes if they formed a *burgher* corps; whether they might form a "*laager*" (place of defence) where they liked within the district, and after receiving satisfactory answers, the spokesman asked that the *burghers* might have "*dree minuten*" to make up their minds. On this the Civil Commissioner and the lieutenant retired; and when they returned to receive the decision, the spokesman announced that the *burghers* had agreed to the Government conditions, the detested drill included.

The Civil Commissioner then administered the oath of allegiance to each *burgher* (as is the custom before any man is admitted into a volunteer or *burgher* corps); and very solemn about it each Boer was, as if he was selling his freedom. "*Ik*, Henricus Johannes Nell, *sweer*," etc., etc.

At the commencement of the swearing-in, the tall young man who spoke first did nothing but fidget about the room, repeating "that he had always been free and didn't want to be made a soldier of, and would *not* be drilled." However, he pushed in amongst the others before half the men had been sworn in, and eventually took the oath quite cheerfully.

The conclusion of the ceremony was three cheers for Her Majesty the Queen, three cheers for His Excellency the Governor, and even one cheer more for the "*offizeer.*"

"The best of those fellows is," said the Civil Commissioner when departing, "that although it is hard to lead them and impossible to drive them, when they once give their word they always stick to it."

The lieutenant has yet a hundred and fifty miles or so to travel before he completes his work.

He has now to leave Eland's Post and the pleasant Amatola Mountains, and has to reach Fort Beaufort, then descend to the dried-up country between the Kat and Koonap Rivers, toil up to the Koonap heights only to descend into the deep Brak River valley, then wind up the baboon-haunted Queen's Road, before he reaches Graham's Town and can turn his horse's head towards King William's Town again.

He hears the same story, and sees the same sights everywhere— colonists, town bred or country bred, coming forward cheerfully to fight for their country; deserted farms; stock dying for want of water; trade at almost a standstill; farmers, who are not away fighting, gloomy and depressed, as they are losing much stock by theft and by the long drought, and the land wanting rain so badly that if they can manage to overcome its hardness and drive the plough through it, the seed-corn dies in the ground.

We must, however, leave the lieutenant to complete his journey, and return to King William's Town, where events are marching fast.

CHAPTER 4

The War Concluded

Shortly after the outbreak of hostilities with Kreli (it is hoped that it is understood that Kreli is chief of the Galekas, and lives in the "Transkei"), Mapassa, one of Kreli's chiefs, declared for Government; and as his brother chiefs threatened to make short work of him and his men if they could get at him, he and his followers and their possessions were escorted across the Kei into the colony, and placed near a place called "Impetu," about forty miles distant from King William's Town.

Here, while the Galekas were flying to the Bashee, Mapassa and his men managed to make the time pass without its hanging too heavily on their hands, by visiting their friends the Gaikas, by a little stock-stealing, and so forth; and here they were when it became very clear, about the beginning of December, that the Galekas were not yet crushed, but were returning into their old country, having deposited their women, children, and cattle in safety, to give battle again.

In order to prevent any of Mapassa's people changing their minds and joining in the disturbance across the Kei, it was determined that they should be disarmed.

Indeed, it was more than suspected that the fashionable young bloods of Mapassa's and even Sandilli's people were in the practice of going off to enjoy a day's shooting with Kreli, returning to their homes to assume, with considerable swagger, the enviable position of a warrior who has blooded his *assegais*—or, as we should say who has "smelt powder."

A party of police and volunteers was accordingly sent down to carry out the disarmament, but it was not cleverly managed.

Mapassa's men had been allowed to hear of the intention to disarm them some days before it was carried into effect, and consequently they had full time to think about it.

Among Mapassa's petty chiefs there was a gentleman named Mackinnon, who was a Gaika by blood. His antecedents would not bear much looking into: his youth had been somewhat stormy; he had made the colony too hot to hold him, and had gone to live with the Galekas across the River Kei.

When Mackinnon heard that Government was going to disarm him and his men, he determined to evade this operation, and accordingly marched away from Impetu, and hid among his relatives the Gaikas.

As soon as Government received news of Mackinnon's flight, a special commissioner was sent to Sandilli, the Gaika chief, and secured from him a promise to surrender Mackinnon, and that a fine should be inflicted upon his people.

This was the most anxious time of the whole war. It was evident that the rising could no longer be regarded as a mere affair of police, to be settled without the aid of Her Majesty's troops, and that if we were to retain our hold on Ibeka, round which the Galekas were again beginning to swarm, reinforcements must be at once sent there; it was evident, too, that the Gaikas really meant mischief, and that the only way by which they could be kept from rising was by dealing the Galekas a rapid and a severe blow.

Unfortunately, at no time since the commencement of the war had the Government been so powerless. Most of the volunteers who had accompanied Commandant Griffith had returned home, the police horses were worn out, and we had not a soldier to spare without too much reducing the force at some important post.

Negotiations were still dragging on between the Government and Sandilli, when, on the 3rd of December, the Galekas had returned to their old country in sufficient force to justify Kreli's ablest and most determined general, Kiva, in making a vigorous attack upon a body of police and volunteers who were patrolling about fifteen miles from Ibeka, in an enclosed and rugged bit of country. The force only numbered twenty-five mounted police and about one hundred and twenty-five volunteers, with two field-pieces. After a brisk skirmish of about half an hour the colonists retired into a more open part of the country, and formed camp, where they were shortly after attacked by between eight and nine hundred warriors.

After a fight which lasted from four to eight o'clock p.m., during which the little force behaved very gallantly, and the two field-pieces did great execution, the Galekas retired, sweeping off the horses and draught oxen of the colonists.

This action was regarded by the Kafirs as a victory, and its effects were speedily seen; for on the 24th of December, Kiva, with two hundred picked men, crossed the Kei into the colony and passed into the Gaika location.

It was no longer doubtful that the Gaikas intended to rise, and the excitement in the colony was at its height.

The disturbances and fighting had hitherto been confined to the Transkei, but now, unfortunately, the colony was to have its share.

On Christmas Day, Sandilli, with great consideration and perhaps some kindly feeling towards the man at whose house he had enjoyed so many pleasant drinking bouts, sent warning to the owner of the hotel and store at Draibosch (a station about thirty-five miles on the main road between King William's Town and the Transkei), telling him to "*trek*," as he proposed to burn his place the next night.

The Draibosch hotel and store was accordingly sacked and burnt, and news was spread through the colony that the Gaikas had at last broken out, and that our communications with the Transkei were cut off.

On the 29th of December, Major Moore, of the 88th Connaught Rangers (who had been placed in command of the mounted police), started from Komgha, a village and military post about forty miles from King William's Town, with about thirty men of the mounted police, to escort the post-riders to Kei Road station—the railway terminus. The force was attacked by three hundred Kafirs. The police dismounted and commenced firing, but owing to most of them being but half trained, and their horses half broken, and also to their being so few in number they were forced to retire, and were closely pressed by the Kafirs. One of the police being awkward at mounting, Major Moore rode back to assist him just as the Kafirs were surrounding him. Major Moore shot three Kafirs with his revolver, received an *assegai* thrust through his arm, and had his horse also wounded; and then, and not till then, and when he saw that the unfortunate policeman had been stabbed to death, did he think of his own safety.

The result of this skirmish was very inspiriting to the Kafirs, who assembled the next day on the same road to have another tussle with the white man.

It was evident that another effort must be at once made to reopen communications with the Transkei, as along the road now closed by the enemy every ounce of flour and every cartridge had to pass.

37

Luckily the natives had a superstitious dread of the telegraph (the lightning poles as they are called in Kafir), and all that appertained to it; regarding the whole contrivance as an important fetish of the white man's, which it would be well not to annoy or meddle with.

On the 30th of December Major Moore, and forty of the 88th Regiment and thirty police, set out from Komgha with this object. He had not advanced far before the war-cry was heard, and the dusky figures of the enemy seen in large numbers on the adjacent hills, and his advanced patrols were soon in contact with the enemy.

He posted his men on some rising ground where some large boulders afforded partial cover, and here they were shortly attacked by between six and seven hundred Kafirs.

The 88th Regiment had only lately come out from England, and, having been suddenly made up to its strength for foreign service, was composed almost entirely of boys.

Boys as they were, and some of them hardly knowing how to fire off their rifles, the forty Connaught Rangers Major Moore had with him fully sustained the old reputation of their corps. Their firing, however, was wild and rapid, and (the bullocks of the ammunition cart having proved traitors, and having hurried away with their load directly the firing commenced) cartridges began to get scarce; upon which Major Moore, whenever the Kafirs got unpleasantly near the position, ordered bayonets to be fixed, and charged out with his gallant little band of redcoats, amongst whom were some of the more sombrely clad frontier police; and the Kafirs, with their traditional dread of coming to close quarters with the "red devils," drew back each time a charge was made.

After about an hour and a half's fighting the Kafirs withdrew leisurely, and, remembering perhaps their theory of the uselessness of trying to take any post from the soldiers, left their sixty odd antagonists in possession of their hill and their boulders.

The Kafirs who had fought in the old wars laid it down as an axiom that if the "*amasoja*", (the Kafir adaptation of "soldier") were in some position and wanted to hold it, or the Kafirs were in some position and the redcoats wanted to take it, it was no use in either case struggling against their desires, for the "red devils" would fight on till they got what they wanted. But there were two things the soldiers could not do: they could not march, and they could not shoot. Since the Kafirs have found out the difference between Brown Bess and the Martini-Henry, they say it's no good fighting, as the soldiers "can shoot them out of another world"—alluding to the long range and the new weapon.

This action had the good effect of clearing the road and opening communications with the Transkei, which were never afterwards interfered with.

From that day the prospects of the colony seemed to brighten, and a fortnight later we were in a position to resume the offensive.

The welcome news had arrived that a battery of artillery and a battalion of foot were on their way to aid us.

The great exertions which had been made since the beginning of December to induce volunteers to come forward were now beginning to bear fruit, and scarcely a day passed without detachments of mounted *burghers*—big, hardy men, dressed in corduroy suits and broad-brimmed hats—or bodies of *Fingo* levies, arriving at King William's Town, to be equipped and forwarded as soon as possible to join one of the columns which were being formed on different parts of the frontier for the chastisement of the Kafirs.

In addition to the volunteer and *burgher* corps, there were three semi-regular corps raised, without which the general commanding would have been put to great straits for men who could be sent here and there, without any question being raised as to whether they were willing to go or not. These corps were the Diamond Fields Horse, under Captain Warren, R.E.; the Frontier Light Horse, under Lieutenant Carrington, 24th Regiment; and the Rangers, under Colonel Pulleine, 24th Regiment The first two numbered about two hundred men each, and the last corps about four hundred men, and all three corps proved most valuable during the war.

From the third week in January, 1878, until the end of the first week in February, operations were prosecuted with great vigour against the Kafirs, not only against those who were swarming in the vicinity of the Kei, but also against Gongubella's Tambookie Kafirs, in the neighbourhood of Queen's Town.

The colonists, commanded by Commandants Griffith, Brabant, and Frost, were everywhere successful, and showed how safe the honour of the colony was in their hands. Owing to the extremely rugged country, and in some instances to differences of opinion between commanders, the operations of the different columns did not perhaps display as much combination as could have been wished; but the Kafirs were getting the worst of it on all sides, and after a determined effort for victory by the combined forces of Kreli and Sandilli on the 7th of

February, they seemed to be almost resigned to defeat, and fought in desperation without hope of success, and because they were ordered to fight by their chiefs.

On the 7th of February, Captain Upcher, 24th Regiment, in command of a camp which had been lately formed in the Transkei, at Quintana Mountain, about twelve miles from Ibeka, was attacked by a force of between five and six thousand Kafirs.

Captain Upcher's force consisted of about four hundred Europeans and five hundred and fifty *Fingoes*, two mountain guns, and a rocket tube. Of the four hundred Europeans, twenty-five were bluejackets, from Her Majesty's ship *Active*, two hundred belonged to Her Majesty's 24th Regiment, ninety were mounted police, seventy were from the Frontier Light Horse, and the volunteers of the colony were ably represented by a gun detachment of the Cape Town Volunteer Artillery.

The enemy advanced to the attack about 3.30 a.m., and some of the 24th and of the Frontier Light Horse were sent forward to commence the action, with orders to retire in haste before the enemy, so as to draw them on and bring them within range of the camp, where suitable preparations for their reception had been made.

Much encouraged by the sudden retreat of the soldiers, the Kafirs advanced in two divisions from two points of the compass, and a third party attempted a surprise by making use of a wooded *kloof* (*Anglicè*, ravine) to the right front of the camp.

The enemy was, however, by 10.30 a.m. driven back on all sides with very heavy loss, and was in full retreat, pursued by Carringon's horse, the mounted police, and the *Fingo* levies.

The Kafirs lost very heavily; about two hundred bodies were found in the open, and many must have fallen in the long grass and in the *kloofs*. The number of wounded must also have been considerable.

Lest some Galeka or Gaika warrior peruse these lines and be inclined to accuse the paleface scribbler of undue partiality in his account of this action, we will give the story of the fight in the words of a Gaika warrior, as told *vivâ voce* to a colonist shortly after it had taken place:—

> Kreli and Sandilli met near the Quintana Mountain and consulted as to what they should do next. Kreli wanted to attack the camp, but Sandilli said, 'No! No good will come of it. Let us rather sweep through *Fingo* Land, where no white men are, and carry off the cattle of the dogs (*Fingoes*), and retreat with

them into the rough country, where none can follow.' But Kreli and his counsellors still said they would attack the camp. Kreli assembled his fighting men and spoke big words to them.

'He, Kreli, the old tree, who had shadowed them so long, stood before them that day. He was the tree their fathers had lain under, safe and sheltered, and for whom their fathers had often fought the white man. Today they could show if they were the white man's dogs, or if they were their fathers' sons.'

Then the Galeka army advanced, led by Kiva and Sigeau" (the two most enterprising Galeka generals), "but the Gaikas were held back by Sandilli. Then we saw that, as the Galikas came on, the soldiers ran, holding their boxes at their backs with one hand; then we, the Gaikas, shouted that the white man was running, and that we too must help to beat the soldiers, and we would not listen to Sandilli and his words.

We joined in the attack, and ran on towards the white soldiers' camp, until we came near to a little ditch in which the soldiers were lying quite quiet. Then came a blaze: our men fell like grass. We saw no more; we ran; our men fell fast, and our hopes were gone. Sandilli and we Gaikas fled across the Kei into our own country, and Kreli and his fighting men took refuge in a hiding-place in Galeka Land."

Our loss was trifling—two men killed, nine wounded, and four horses killed.

It was now, notwithstanding the reverses of their compatriots, that the war spirit seemed to gain such irresistible influence over so many civilized Kafirs. Kafirs who had been Christians since their boyhood, who had worn clothes and lived in houses all their lives—well-educated men, speaking and writing English with admirable correctness—who, perhaps, were holding good appointments as clerks or interpreters under Government—would yield to the feeling, and, urged by a desire for fighting and excitement, and by loyalty to their chiefs, would leave their situations, exchange their clothes for a blanket, their pen for a rifle, and join their tribe in the bush.

The idea that because a Kafir changes his religion he therefore at the same time changes (what may be called) his politics, hardly seems a reasonable one. At any rate, as it turned out, whether a man declared for or against Government depended in most cases upon the line of conduct followed by his chief, and not upon his professing or not professing Christianity. A Gaika chief named Dukwana, the only chief of any importance who had attempted to make Christianity the religion of his clan, after wavering for some time, at last threw in his lot with Sandilli, and joined the native army with his followers.

Dukwana, it is said, not only retained his European dress in the bush, but held service regularly, at which he compelled the attendance of all the Kafirs under him, whether professing Christianity or not.

History is not wanting in examples of conquered peoples accepting the religion, but revolting against the government, of their conquerors; and it cannot be denied that the missionaries, by leading the colonists to expect that a native having once embraced Christianity will become English in his sympathies, pave the way for a deplorable reaction of opinion as to the value of Christianity for the natives when this error is exposed.

During the first week of February the promised battery and the 90th Light Infantry arrived, and were right welcome. These troops were despatched, almost immediately after landing, to garrison Fort Beaufort, near which a Gaika chief named Tini Macomo had just (at the wrong time for him and the right time for us) declared against Government.

The rest of February was spent in preparing for operations against Tini Macomo and against Sandilli, who was now posted in some very rugged and difficult country near the Thomas River, an affluent of the Kei.

On the 4th of March Colonel Palmer, 90th Light Infantry, with a mixed force of regulars, and *burghers*, and native levies, attacked Tini Macomo, who was ensconced in the depths of the Schelm and Water *Kloofs* (of evil notoriety from the losses our troops had suffered therein during past wars), and in a few days' time succeeded in driving out the Kafirs and restoring confidence in the town and district of Fort Beaufort.

At this time there were two main columns in the Transkei—one composed of regulars and *Fingo* levies, under Colonel Glyn; another of police and Tembu levies, under Major Elliott, a retired Crimean officer, who was Resident with the Tembus, and whose firm and prompt action induced this tribe to declare for, and render much valuable assistance to, Government during the war. There was, however, but little doing in Galeka Land—the Galekas who remained there apparently being cowed and preferring to remain in hiding.

Early in March, however, a body of *Fingoes*, under a European officer, attacked one of the hiding-places, and in the fighting which then ensued the celebrated Kiva and several minor chiefs were killed.

On the 9th of March Sandilli succeeded in breaking away from Commandant Griffith's forces, who were endeavouring to surround him on the Thomas River, and making his way into a part of the Amatola Mountains called the Buffalo Range.

The second battalion, 24th Regiment, opportunely arrived from England just at this time, and were hurried up to participate in a general attack on Sandilli's forces.

The troops engaged were 555 regulars, 1185 mounted volunteers, 1295 native levies, and four mountain guns, and there was continuous fighting from the 18th to the 21st of March, and smaller actions for ten days afterwards. The result of this fortnight's work was not as decisive as could have been wished, though it may at first sight appear that the Kafirs should have been almost annihilated by so persistent an attack. But the ruggedness and difficult nature of the ground rendered our task of very great difficulty, and the enemy, by taking refuge in the deep *kloofs*, bush-covered ravines, and thick-wooded recesses of the hills, were enabled to hold out still against us.

The only breathing time that the Kafirs had for nearly three months was for the first three weeks of April, during which time Seyolo, a Gaika chief, with nearly twelve hundred men, took the opportunity of rising, and joined Sandilli's forces.

The general commanding (General Thesiger) was forced to suspend hostilities at this juncture, as the time for which the volunteers and *burghers* under his command had enrolled had expired; and they had to be dismissed to their homes and men to relieve them obtained.

On the 29th of April offensive operations were resumed.

It would make too long a story to recount in detail the operations directed by General Thesiger during the remainder of April, and during May and June. Suffice it to say that the operations were conducted with a vigour and an energy generally unknown in the old Kafir wars.

The enemy, owing to the care with which his haunts were watched, had been brought to great straits for food and ammunition, and the Kafirs were also suffering from the cold.

There was almost continued fighting for the first ten days of May, during which the Kafirs lost heavily, and it began to be evident that resistance must soon cease.

The operations during the remainder of May dwindled down to

a succession of small combats between the troops and parties of half-starved and desperate men, who would not give, themselves up, but who only fought when they could neither hide nor escape.

This was not at all the sort of warfare their chiefs and the old warriors of their tribes, who had fought in previous Kafir wars, had led them to expect.

They had intended to rise suddenly, take the English unawares, sweep off plenty of cattle and sack farmhouses, and away to the mountains with their booty. From their vantage point they had intended, as in previous wars, to make raids on the surrounding country in one direction, while the troops toiled wearily after them in another. Then, when they had eaten up their stolen cattle, and had had enough of excitement and of bush life, the chiefs would open negotiations, which would be accepted by a Government sick of the war, and a peace would be speedily patched up.

But this war all had been very different; and now the officers of Government, instead of agreeing to the terms offered by the Kafirs, demanded immediate submission to their terms.

On the 29th of May an important event occurred. Sandilli, the great chief of the fighting Gaikas, the drunken and treacherous old savage who had brought so much misery upon his own people and the colonists of the frontier, was killed by a stray shot; and his bodyguard were so hard pressed that they could not carry off his body, but had only time to throw a few leaves over it.

No operations of any importance took place from this date, and on the 29th of June an amnesty to all who would lay down, their arms was proclaimed, and the war was virtually at an end.

The losses of the Kafirs by far exceeded those of any of the former Kafir wars. Of the Gaikas all the most important chiefs were killed—Sandilli and several of his sons, Dukwana, Seyolo, and many others. Tini Macomo, Edmund Sandilli (Sandilli's chief son,) Gongubella, chief of the Tambookies, were taken prisoners. Of the Galekas, Kreli, the prime mover of the war, was a fugitive, hunted about from place to place with a handful of followers. Kiva, Sigeau, and many other Galeka chiefs and counsellors were dead.

Yet, although the Kafirs had suffered so severely by the war, and had been so thoroughly beaten, they did not seem inclined to settle down. There was still that curious spirit of unrest abroad, which had urged them to take up arms, and though they had no longer the power of active resistance, yet they seemed sullenly defiant.

The wave of disturbance which had been sweeping the huge area from the Limpopo to the Orange River and to the Kei since, in 1876, the Transvaal Boers had had to retire from Sekukuni's stronghold, had not yet subsided, and did not seem to be subsiding.

What was it that kept alive the war spirit, and that prevented the Eastern frontier Kafirs settling down and resuming their peaceful avocations after so much trouble and hardship? The reason was this. They were looking eastwards for help and sympathy—eastwards, where dwelt a great and much-dreaded king, who styled himself in his secret diplomatic intrigues, and was believed by many to be, more powerful than the great white Queen, who had never yet been seen, and whose soldiers, though they could fight, seemed so very few in number.

Some of the English papers have accused the South Africans of having the disease of Cetywayo on the brain, and have asserted that the smallest occurrence could not take place without it being considered that the Zulu king was at the bottom of it.

In the offices of many a Civil Commissioner on the Eastern frontier, amongst the dusty records of the Native-Affairs Bureaux at Cape Town, at Maritzburg, and at Pretoria, would be found many interesting documents and reports from anxious border or native magistrates, who, though hundreds of miles apart, would seem to have suffered severely from this curious disease. In these offices would be found overwhelming evidence to prove that wherever in South Africa trouble was, wherever magistrates reported uneasiness or discontent among the natives, wherever a native rising took place, there was to be found Cetywayo's influence at work.

It did not much matter where the trouble was. On the banks of the Vaal, where the Matabele (as the Zulus are there called) would have a difficulty in making themselves understood; in the Cape Colony, amongst the Amatola Mountains; in the rocky fastnesses of Basuto Land; in the arid country bordering on the great Orange River; in the broken hills and *krantzes* of Sekukuni's mountains—no matter where or upon what pretext the trouble began, the Zulu king's handiwork could be discerned. Magistrates hundreds of miles apart would report almost on the same day to headquarters, and the pith of their reports would be the same: Zulus had been found concealed in the neighbourhood; they (perhaps) had been seized; when questioned as to their movements, they said they were not sent by anybody—they were trading; they had come to buy skins, or hunting dogs, *or* guns, etc., etc.; they did not know the white men did not like natives travelling about their country without leave; they were sorry if they had done wrong, and would go back to Zulu Land if they might: and then would probably follow an unfavourable report concerning the attitude of the natives in the neighbourhood of the writer.

So it became evident, months—nay, years—before the Kafir rising of 1877, that there was a bad spirit towards the white man abroad. It seemed as if the natives, from one end of South Africa to the other, had come to think that there was a decisive time rapidly approaching, when the black man would be able to measure strength again with the white man—when the black man would make one more effort to recover his country from the white man. Cetywayo, the great king, was with them, and had encouraged his dog, Sekukuni, to attack the white man; and, look, he was not yet beaten.

The white man had taken the country, and had conquered before by being so well armed with guns. Now they had guns and could meet the white man on nearly equal terms, and if they waited on the words of the Zulu king, and attacked the white man when he told them, the white man would be destroyed.

This was the strain of native political reasoning, and there were few *kraals* of any importance in South Africa in which Zulu diplomats had not urged the anti-white man policy on its owners. Thus, the attitude of the tribes throughout South Africa was one of sullen expectancy. "Yes, you have beaten us," said an old Galeka warrior to a native magistrate. "You have beaten us well, but there," said he, pointing eastward—"there are the Ama Zulu warriors! Can you beat them? They say not! Go and try. Don't trouble any more about us, but beat *them*, and we shall be quiet enough,"

When the operations against Sekukuni had to be brought to a close without his having been subdued, on account of the commencement of the sickly season, the saying went abroad among the native tribes: "If the bull-calf [Sekukuni] has to be let alone, what will happen when the elephant [Cetywayo] attacks the white man?"

CHAPTER 5

Zulus

Some few years after the beginning of this century, the lands east of the Great Bashee River—what we now call Pondo Land, Natal, and Zulu Land—lying below the mountain chain of the Drakensberg (so named from the dragons the first Dutch "*foretrekkers* "declared they saw sitting on the mountain peaks when they first penetrated into the country), were inhabited by various small tribes, who lived in tolerably peaceful relations to each other. The Zulus were only a small tribe living somewhere in the neighbourhood of Cetywayo's old *kraal*, Undini.

About the time when this century had reached its second decade great changes began to take place. A new king of the Zulu tribe was placed on the throne. Determined, ambitious, warlike, far-seeing, crafty, insatiably bloodthirsty, Chaka soon changed the face of the surrounding country.

Bent on conquest, he began his reign by manufacturing an army, and, by the severest code of discipline conceivable, he succeeded in turning his people into admirable soldiers.

Chaka formed his able-bodied male population into regiments, forbade his young men to marry without his leave, and built military *kraals*, which answered the same purpose as barracks in improving the discipline of his men. His system of training and discipline was admirable for the object he had in view. For the least disobedience or symptom of wavering in performing a duty, death was the punishment inflicted.

Chaka laid the foundation of the system of Zulu tactics, of which we shall speak later on. His men were armed with a shield of cowhide of oval shape—each regiment having its distinctive colour—and with three *assegais*, two throwing and one stabbing *assegai*. It was death for

47

a Zulu soldier to lose his stabbing spear.

His army being formed, drilled, and disciplined, Chaka soon began to test its prowess.

His warriors, having once conquered, became irresistible. Even those amongst them who had no natural taste for fighting fought with the heroism of desperation; for they knew that even if they managed, by evading their fair share of fighting, to elude the enemy's weapons, a worse fate awaited them.

There is still pointed out in Zulu Land, near Undini, a round bush, called by the Zulus, "The Coward's Bush." It looks an ordinary bush enough, but it has witnessed many a bloody ceremony. Here it was that Chaka used to review his troops on their return from an expedition. Here it was he meted out praise and blame to his captains and their men, his army being drawn up in a huge semicircle round him. Then, after saying what he would to them, he would order the regiments in turn to march past, and as each regiment arrived at a certain spot and was in a suitable formation, the king's order was given, "Bring forth your cowards," and the poor wretches who had shown signs of wavering or slackness in fighting, were brought out and put an end to.

Chaka then made war on all sides of him, and with rapid success. At first, seeing that his army was not sufficiently numerous, all tried warriors of other tribes who submitted to his rule and accepted his military discipline were spared. This, however, was in the early days of his career. Soon he found he had warriors enough, and the fiat went forth that no quarter was to be given to man, woman, or child, to warrior, maiden, suckling, or dotard; and this has remained, since Chaka's time, one of the standing orders of a Zulu *impi*.

Chaka, then, was the founder of the national feeling among the Zulus, who, before this time, were only an unimportant clan; from his ascending the throne they date their military reputation and their superiority over all other Kafir tribes. Chaka, after making his name known and dreaded from the Maputa to the Great Fish River, was assassinated on the 28th of September, and the treacherous and wily Dingaan ascended the throne. Dingaan, after a reign writ in letters of blood, was in 1840 driven from Zulu Land by the Dutch, and was killed by the Amaswazi (whose land lies north and north-west of Zulu Land). With Dingaan's death the independence of the Zulus virtually disappeared. The Dutch placed a king of their own choosing on the throne, Panda, a brother of Chaka and Dingaan, and from 1840, the year in which he was placed on the throne, until 1872, the year of his death, Panda always behaved as dependent on the then existing Government, whether Dutch (which it was to 1846) or English.

Panda was considered a degenerate Zulu; he only killed as many people as would preserve a moderate amount of discipline amongst them. He was no soldier, preferring a quiet life, with the society of his wives and good living, to the sterner pleasures of war, the chase, or political intrigue, which were so much relished by his brothers.

Panda died in 1872, and the chief nobles and princes of the Zulu nation reported the king's death officially to the Lieutenant-Governor of Natal, and begged that the great Queen's Government would now finally install Cetywayo, Panda's son, who had been nominated some years before to succeed his father as King of the Zulus.

The British Government assented, and Sir Theophilus Shepstone was sent to place Cetywayo on the throne; the massacres which generally took place when a Zulu king was crowned being forbidden by the British Government, who also distinctly ordered that the indiscriminate shedding of blood was to cease, that no Zulu should be killed without fair trial, and the king's sanction should be necessary before any Zulu was put to death. Cetywayo formally accepted the terms on which the British Government would consent to place him on the throne, and he was accordingly crowned and proclaimed King of the Zulus.

It soon was evident that there was now on the throne a man worthy indeed to be king, if gauged by the military standard of a Zulu brave. To a considerable part of the military abilities and all the ambition of Chaka, Cetywayo added the craftiness and unscrupulous cruelty of Dingaan, and he did not allow these qualities, abilities, or vices to rust for want of work. Cetywayo, on ascending the throne, hurried forward the completion of the reorganization of the army, to which he had already for many years paid great attention.

Panda, peaceably inclined as he was, paid but little heed to the organization of the army of Chaka and Dingaan, and, until Cetywayo began to be powerful and to use his influence in the matter, the Zulu military system had fallen considerably to pieces.

Cetywayo commenced at once collecting the old regiments and forming new ones, selecting his commanders and subordinate officers with care. He formed numerous military *kraals*, and regularly assembled his regiments for training or exercise. He lost no opportunity of encouraging the military spirit of his army and of strengthening the cords of discipline in his regiments.

Bearing in mind that firearms enabled the Dutch Boers to defeat eventually his uncle Dingaan, he determined that his army should be armed with firearms, and issued the most stringent orders to his commanding officers that their men should be armed with guns. "Have not I once already told you," a trader heard him say to a chief who commanded one of his regiments, "that your men are to have guns? Go! Do you see that place where the grass is burnt? I give you till the grass is so high," putting his hand some two feet from the ground; "beware of seeing my face after that until your men have all guns."

To their discipline Cetywayo paid great attention; death was again the punishment for every offence; the king's nod must be obeyed, no matter what consequences followed. It is difficult to realize the pitch to which this was brought by the king. Not long before the Zulu war broke out, a missionary was expatiating to Cetywayo, who had one of his regiments seated round him, of the danger he ran of hell fire. "Hell fire!" repeated Cetywayo. "Do you frighten me with hell fire? My army would put it out. See!" continued he, pointing to a grass fire which was burning over a considerable tract, and calling to the officer commanding the regiment, "Before you look on me again, eat up that fire," The thousands of which the regiment were composed were in an instant bounding, shouting the war-cry, towards the fire, which was eaten up without regard to those who were maimed and permanently damaged.

Cetywayo revived and elaborated the tactics of Chaka.

The Zulu attack formation was composed of three divisions—two horns, BB, and a main body or chest, C; there was also a reserve, D, who were supposed to be seated with their faces away from the enemy, A, so as not to be excited or influenced in any way by the operations of the main body.

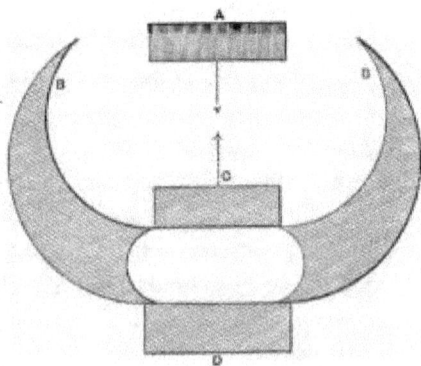

An attack being ordered, the two horns are sent out to attack the flanks and rear of the enemy, and when these or one of them has made good their advance, the chest of the army advances and completes the victory. At feasts and gala occasions, reviews by the king, and so on, the regiments parade in all their pomp of war—skins, feathers, etc., each regiment having its distinctive badges; but for service all this is laid aside. *Assegais*, rifle, shield and ammunition, and a sort of kilt of skin are all the Zulu warrior carries. Chiefs alone wear head-dresses as distinctive marks.

Next to its perfect discipline, the mobility of the Zulu army is its most remarkable feature.

A Zulu *impi* can cover forty and fifty miles a day, its food and sleeping mats being carried by women.

Nothing can stop a Zulu *impi* on the march. Rough ground is nothing to them; over rocky country the horse must be good and un-tired to beat a Zulu. On coming to a river in flood, an *impi* forms into close order; the men link arms, shout the war-cry, and charge the river as a foe. The weakest go down, but the *impi* gets through.

Such, then, was the Zulu army in 1878. Against whom was this formidable engine to be used? Was it for his amusement that Cety-wayo had turned, like a savage Frederick the Great, his nation into sol-diers? Was it necessary in order to resist the Swazies, or to keep down the Tongas, that he kept up a standing army of fifty thousand men? or had he been fired by ambition, and bitten by the same lust of conquest as his grandfather Chaka?

I may venture to say that all South Africans and all those who have made the burning questions of South Africa their study, with very few exceptions think the last explanation is the one which discovers the policy of the Zulu king.

Though for many years he had done much towards rousing the martial spirit of the nation and towards reforming the army, it was in 1873 that Cetywayo ascended the Zulu throne, a suppliant for Eng-lish favour, and vowing faithfully to keep his promises that his people should have good and fair government, and even reporting the first execution he ordered to Sir Theophilus Shepstone, with an explana-tion as to why he had deemed it necessary to put the man to death.

It would be a long story to show in detail the dexterity with which the Zulu king played off the Dutch of the Transvaal against the Gov-ernment of Natal; how, as he got his army into better order and felt more secure on his throne, his tone grew more and more defiant; how his rule became more and more barbarous, until the Tugela beheld a continuous stream of refugees, who, though they had to leave all their possessions in Zulu Land, preferred to begin life again rather than live under Cetywayo's bloody rule; how, when the English Government forbade the invasion of the Transvaal and then annexed the country, Cetywayo changed his tone and became almost openly hostile. All this, if told in detail, would make too long a story. But to show the adroitness of the Zulu king, and how deeply laid his schemes, I select an extract from a report by the Hon. Charles Brownlee, late Secretary for Native Affairs in the Cape Colony, a gentleman whose character stands justly very high in South Africa, and who possesses the respect and confidence of all classes of colonists and natives. The report is dated November, 1878, and will be found in the South African Blue Book, C. 2222.

Mr. Brownlee, after a short sketch of the Zulu power, and of Cetywayo's succession to the throne, says, "While professing friendship for us, Cetywayo's support and countenance are found on the side of our enemies. Between Moshesh [the supreme chief of the Basutos] and Panda, friendly relationships had long existed. Shortly after the surrender of Langalibalele to us by Molapo, Moshesh's second son in rank, Molapo, as in the days of his father and the days of Cetywayo's father, sent an embassy to Cetywayo to condole with him on the death of Panda, and to congratulate him on his accession to the Zulu monarchy.

Molapo's messengers were not permitted to approach Cetywayo. He directed that they should be driven back with indignity from the borders of Zulu Land, from whence their advance had been announced, and they were directed to inform Molapo that he had made himself a traitor to the coloured races by surrendering Langalibalele to the white men, and that Cetywayo would be revenged upon him. This was about a year after his installation by us, and while he was professing the greatest friendship towards us.

In conclusion, I may remark that Cetywayo's hand has been clearly traced in our recent troubles on the Cape frontier, as well as in the Transvaal.

In July or August, 1877, Umquikela [Chief of the' Pondos] wrote to the High Commissioner, expressing his willingness to obey the decision of his Excellency in regard to the surrender of the murderers in the matter of Somfu Land; at the same time Sekukuni was cheerfully paying his war indemnity to the Transvaal Government. Cetywayo, however, appears on the scene, and matters are changed.

To Umquikela a deputation is sent, and from information received it appears that the mission was for the establishment of friendly relations with the Pondos, with a promise of aid from Cetywayo in case the Pondos should come into conflict with us, and it was further reported that the Pondos had been urged to comply with none of our demands,

After the deputation had been in Pondo Land for about three months, Umquikela having reported nothing to us regarding Cetywayo's messages, I, by direction of the High Commissioner, wrote to Umquikela to inform him of what we had heard, expressing surprise that he should receive such overtures from the Zulus, who, till our intervention, had destroyed the Pondos, and would do so again did we permit it. Umquikela denied that Cetywayo had sent any overtures hostile to us, but stated that Cetywayo's messengers had simply been sent to beg for skins and dogs.

This may have been the pretext, but it is by no means likely that it was the true object of the mission, which was prolonged three or four months. At any rate, during the stay of Cetywayo's messengers, Umquikela, notwithstanding the promise contained in his letter to the High Commissioner, absolutely refused to surrender the murderers who had fled from justice in Natal, and who were then in his country.

At the same time Kreli, who had been personally opposed to taking up arms against the Government, suddenly changed his policy, and had the war paint placed upon his forehead; for it was said the Zulus were coming to aid the Kafirs, and to within a very recent period both Galekas and Gaikas both hoped to obtain aid from this source.

In the Transvaal at the same time the same influences were visible. As has already been remarked, Sekukuni was cheerfully paying his war indemnity, but having received a deputation from Cetywayo with a present of one hundred oxen, Sekukuni suddenly changed his course of action—the payment of the war indemnity ceased, and from thence began the troubles which have led to the present position of the Transvaal, and for this Cetywayo is directly responsible.

To show the difference of tone between Cetywayo with his army half armed and organized, insecure on his throne, and bidding for the friendship of the English Government, and Cetywayo secure in his hold on the people, his army well armed and eager for war, an extract from a message received from the Zulu king by the Lieutenant-Governor of Natal is inserted, which was received at the end of 1876. The message was in reply to a temperately and cautiously worded message from Sir Henry Bulwer, remonstrating with the Zulu king on a wholesale massacre of a number of young women and girls. The Zulu king had, at one of the yearly feasts, given permission to the men of one of his older regiments to marry, and ordered that a certain number of young women and girls should marry them.

These, not fancying the age of their intended husbands, refused, and Cetywayo ordered them all to be killed. This was done, and their bodies strewed in the highways (such as they are) of Zulu Land, to serve as an example to other disobedient subjects. The relatives of some of these unfortunate creatures came and gathered up and buried the remains of their kinswomen. This Cetywayo heard of, and ordered that all who could be caught who had done this should also be killed, and his orders were well obeyed.

Reply of Cetywayo in November, 1876, to message of the Lieutenant-Governor of Natal on the occasion of the massacre of Zulu women in the same year:—

Did I ever tell Somtseu (Shepstone) that I would not kill } Did he tell the white people I made such an arrangement? Because if he did he has deceived them. I *do* kill, but do not consider I have done anything yet in the way of killing. Why do the white people start at nothing? I have not yet begun. I have yet to kill; it is the custom of our nation, and I shall not depart from it.

Why does the Governor of Natal speak to me about my laws? Do I go to Natal and dictate to him about his laws? I shall not agree to any laws and rules from Natal, and by so doing throw the great *kraal* which I govern into the water. My people will not listen unless they are killed, and while wishing to be friends with the English, I do not agree to give my people over to be governed by laws sent to me by them.

Have I not asked the English to allow me to wash my spears since the death of my father, Umpanda, and they have kept playing with me all this time, treating me like a child?

Go back and tell the English that I shall now act on my own account, and if they wish me to agree to their laws, I shall leave and become a wanderer; but before I go it will be seen, as I shall not go without having acted.

Go back and tell the white man this, and let them hear it well! The Governor of Natal and I are equal—he is Governor of Natal, and I am governor here.

In ending this chapter I would remark that these extracts are not intended to prove that the Zulu king is the most dreadful monster and frightful reprobate that ever existed, but to show that he was not the straightforward though cautious, severe but just, patriot ruler, governing his people fairly well according to his lights—shedding blood naturally oftener than a civilized despot, but only as often and not oftener than was necessary to keep his people in order. The true estimate of Cetywayo's character is a common-place and a common-sense one. Long before the Zulu war broke out, the highest authorities on South Africa (except one notable exception, whose following has become smaller year by year), differing as they might on other points, all agreed on one, *viz.*, that the Zulu king was an able, unscrupulous, and extremely ambitious savage, whose possession of a large standing army of young warriors longing for war, was a state of affairs which menaced with ruin the colonies whose border farms and homesteads were within a few hours' march of Cetywayo's capital.

CHAPTER 6

Cetywayo & the Coming War

King William's Town was the best vantage-point from which to see the war on the Cape frontier—for the Zulu war the Transkei must be crossed, and the Bashee River, and then the Umzimvubu or St. John's River, where there is a fine harbour and a little fort, until Pondo Land is reached.

From the boundary of Pondo Land the Umtamvuna River, and thence to Maritzburg, is not far, and it is at Maritzburg we shall be during some part at least of the Zulu war.

When I first knew the pretty little town, with its streets lined with trees, with its streams of water, more or less clear, with its tiled houses and general snug and stay-at-home appearance, it was a very different place to what it was during the war. Then we had a mail about once in five weeks, and its arrival did not excite us very much. We had no telegraph with the Cape or any other colony; we had a telegraph line to the port at Durban, which was very useful when it was not knocked out of order by oxen rubbing themselves against the telegraph poles, an occurrence which took place nearly every other day. There was a scandalous rumour set afloat by evil-disposed persons to the effect that when the telegraph clerks wanted to sleep, or smoke, or play chuck-farthing, or what not, they said "the trek bullocks have put the line out of order;" but this report was most properly discredited by all supporters of Government, and our telegraphic messages from Maritzburg to Durban continued to go as quickly, if not quicker, than letters did by the post-cart.

We used to speculate vaguely how long it would be before the Zulu question would have to be settled, and what would become of Natal if Cetywayo did not give us time to prepare. It was a quiet, pleasant place, where people took it easy and did not "hurry up" at all. Maritzburg, during the Zulu war, was different enough, as will be seen later.

In Natal, since the outbreak of the frontier war in the Cape Colony in September, 1877, events had been moving fast towards war, although everything had been done by the Transvaal and Natal Governments to avert hostilities, for which (were there no other reason against them) we were totally unprepared.

The Natal Government had many causes of complaint against the Zulu king on account of his failure to carry out the promises made at his coronation, but these were not brought forward; nor was it thought advisable by the Natal Government to take notice of the many small acts of insolence or discourtesy by which the Zulu king thought fit to show his changed feelings towards the Government.

Though, however, Cetywayo had no cause of dispute with Natal, there was a long outstanding question with the Transvaal. Between the Buffalo and Pongolo Rivers lay a large tract of land, which the Zulus claimed. The Transvaal Government asserted that it was ceded to the Boers by the Zulus many years before. This the Zulus denied; and up to 1877, though attempts had been made by the Natal Government to act as mediator between the Boers and Zulus, no satisfactory arrangement had been arrived at, on account of the deep-rooted distrust which existed between the claimants.

Peace-loving people, and those who believed in the good intentions of the Zulu king, hoped that the annexation of the Transvaal would pave the way to a speedy solution of this vexed boundary question, as Cetywayo, it was urged, would feel he had now to deal with a Government friendly to him, and one most anxious to do justice to his people.

Cetywayo looked at the matter differently, and shortly after the annexation of the Transvaal marched an *impi* into the disputed territory near the Pongolo River, where a military *kraal* was ordered to be commenced. Zulu messengers also paid visits to many Dutch homesteads, ordering the occupants to leave, and go to land other than that which belonged to their king. It may be imagined how dismayed and terrified the farmers were by this action, which was in reality equivalent to a declaration of war. Many farmers left at once, and trekked away from the Zulu border; and many families were rendered virtually homeless, because, but not through any fault of their own, they had inherited or bought their farms from men whose title to possession was not flawless.

The natives under the British Government in the disputed territory were not better off.

In the mountainous country at the north-west corner of Zulu Land live robber hordes of half-Zulu, half-renegade Swazies. These people, though not considered as part of the Zulu nation, nevertheless owed a sort of allegiance to the Zulu king, and trembled at his nod, or, as a Zulu would say, "were his dogs."

Umbelini, the most important leader of these robber clans, commenced a series of raids into the disputed territory amongst the natives—raids which consisted in killing as many men, women, and children as possible, seizing all the cattle within reach, and retiring into his mountain fastnesses.

The tone of the Transvaal and Natal Governments at this juncture was moderate and conciliatory in the extreme; all that could be done to check matters coming to an extremity was done.

The Natal Government offered to mediate again, and Sir Theophilus Shepstone proceeded from the seat of his government to the Zulu border to attempt an amicable settlement.

The tone of the king's envoys, who were sent to meet Sir Theophilus Shepstone, was most insolent and aggressive. They would not discuss the points at issue, but claimed the land without any compromise. The Zulu king's prime minister was overbearing and defiant; and addressed Sir Theophilus without any of the courtesy titles about which the Zulus are so particular, and at length, winding up by a defiant speech, struck his *assegai* on his shield almost in Sir Theophilus's face, and broke up the meeting without going through any form of leave-taking or farewell.

Yet Sir Theophilus Shepstone did not relax his efforts towards arranging matters, and sent down to Cetywayo one of his sons and the *Landdrost* of Utrecht, a gentleman well known and trusted by the Zulus, who, during these trying times, was continually appealed to for counsel and assistance by the panic-stricken farmers or terrified natives of his district. Mr. Rudolph's story of his last interview with Cetywayo will sound best in his own words:—

"I have met the Zulu king," said he, "four or five times, and know him well. He is a very straightforward man and says out what he thinks. He is not like most of his people. He is very acute and sees the meaning of anything very quickly. I have never believed in his invading Natal. He once said to me, 'If the tiger comes, I will seize him in both hands and crush him, but

I will not go into his country.'

"Cetywayo always treated me kindly, and I think liked and re-spected me, as I always spoke out to him my mind. When I arrived at his *kraal* he always presented me with a fine beast to kill, gave me a good hut, and enough Kafir beer; but the last time was different.

"This was the year before last, after the meeting at Conference Hill of all the Zulu *indunas* and headmen with Sir Theophilus Shepstone, when the meeting broke up abruptly, when Man-yana, the prime minister, had treated Sir Theophilus Shepstone with such discourtesy, calling him by his Zulu name of '*Somt-seu*' short, and never saying '*Inkoss*' when addressing him, and suddenly breaking up the meeting by striking his *assegai* defi-antly on his shield and departing without saying 'farewell.'

"This time Cetywayo treated me unkindly. Henrique Shep-stone and I were sent down to tell the king the terms of the decision of Sir Theophilus Shepstone with regard to the Zulu claims in Transvaal. Shepstone did not wish to sleep at Ceta-wayo's great place. I think he was a little uncertain as to his re-ception, so he slept at the mission station. When he approached the great *kraal*—it is a grand place, eight or nine hundred yards round—a Zulu came out to us, and told us to leave our horses at the entrance and walk. This was a deliberate slight put upon us, and I saw things would not go well.

"We advanced towards the king, who was sitting on a native chair, with Zulus holding shields (not an umbrella) over him to keep off the sun. The king would use nothing European that day. It was very hot. When we came near I saw that there were no seats. Shepstone stood still, but I moved to where I saw Manyana, and asked him for a seat. 'Did you give us seats at Conference Hill?' said he, with a sneering smile. 'What are you walking about for?' said the king, when I returned to where the royal chair was. 'I walk, O son of Umpanda! for, as you know, it is against the rules of your people to remain standing before you, yet you send us not seats.' 'Look,' said the king, 'this *Chèla*' (my name among the Zulus) 'he is a man, he moves about; but this son of Somtseu—what is he? he stands still.' He then ordered mats to be placed on one side and not in a place of honour.

"Before the king allowed us to speak he asked why we had not slept at the royal *kraal*. 'How have I always treated you?' said he. 'Have I not always treated you well, *Chèla*, when you have come to see me? Why then did you not sleep at my *kraal*?' I said that as horse sickness was very prevalent, and the grass round the royal *kraal* not good, we thought it more prudent to keep at the missionaries'. On this the king ordered someone to bring him a handful of a certain poisonous grass. 'Here, feed your horses on this; it will not harm them,' said he. This was to show he did not believe the excuse.

"He was difficult to deal with that day. When Shepstone began speaking he addressed the king as 'Cetywayo.' The king stopped him. Are you the son of only an *induna* to speak to me like that' So Henrique Shepstone said he was in error, and proceeded.

"Then I spoke. I called him 'Cetywayo' first, then 'King of the Zulus' or 'Son of Umpanda,' and then again 'Cetywayo.' He then put out his hand towards me. 'You heard,' he said, 'the word I spoke to that son there of Somtseu. I meant it also for you, yet you have since called me "Cetywayo."' I said, 'You must forgive me, O son of Umpanda, but I—I have known you well, and have so often so called you that my tongue slipped.' Our talk did no good. When we departed, the king pointed out a small beast, to us: 'There, you may take that beast; go, eat it with the missionaries.'"

While the Transvaal Government, as represented by Sir Theophilus Shepstone, were doing their utmost to at least stave off, if it were impossible to altogether avert, the evil day when hostilities should become inevitable, the Natal Government, as represented by Sir Henry Bulwer, were also doing their best towards the same end.

Cetywayo at last consented to refer the matter to the arbitration of the Natal Government, and early in 1878 a commission composed of three gentlemen, two of whom were officials of high rank in the Natal civil service, and the third an officer of the army, of much talent and great energy, commenced its labours.

It would be tedious to go through the pros and cons of a complicated land question. Suffice it to say that the Zulu claim to the land rested on the conquests of Chaka, and they denied having ceded it to the Dutch; and the Dutch claim rested on various real or imaginary cessions of tracts of land by the Zulu rulers. The commission, after having taken what evidence they considered necessary, and after riding hurriedly through portions of the disputed boundary, returned to Maritzburg to draw up their report.

While the commissioners were thus labouring to do justice to the Zulu claims, the attitude of the Zulus continued to give the greatest anxiety throughout Natal and the Transvaal.

Zulus on the border were becoming daily more insolent, and the young men of Cetywayo's best regiments more and more anxious to blood their *assegais* and emulate the deeds of their forefathers. The Natal natives were terrified by threats shouted across the river Tugela to them, and it was altogether evident that a grave crisis was fast approaching. Yet the efforts of the Natal Government were unremitting to let no chance pass of smoothing matters and lessening the tension which every day was becoming more apparent.

So much was this the case that the Lieutenant- Governor of Natal was almost averse to troops being moved to strategic positions, where they could best protect the colony, lest this action should be taken as a menace by the Zulu king.

Towards the latter part of July an occurrence took place which still further complicated matters.

Two women fled from Zulu Land to Natal. They were followed by a brother and two sons of an important chief named Sirayo. These men entered British territory with an armed party, took the two women prisoners, and carried them back again into Zulu Land, where they killed them.

To all those versed in Kafir and Zulu politics, it became more than ever clear that the Zulu king meant war.

The outbreak of a native war is not like the commencement of a war between two civilized Powers. The former is often brought about by some occurrence comparatively insignificant, which, to those who are experts, is decisive warning enough of what will follow.

This violation of British territory, grave enough as it looked in itself, was infinitely graver when considered with all the other occurrences which were taking place.

Redress was demanded in a most temperate message by the Lieutenant-Governor of Natal. Cetywayo sent answer, treating the matter lightly, and disregarding the demand for the surrender of the offenders to be tried by a British court, making different excuses, saying that Sirayo's sons had run away and could not be found—an answer which might not seem ridiculous to people in Europe, but which would have appeared so to those on the spot, who knew the strict discipline maintained by the Zulu king throughout his dominions, had not the situation not been so full of anxiety and peril.

Redress was twice again demanded in August by the Lieutenant-Governor, and again evaded by Cetywayo,

At length, towards the end of November, a message was sent to Cetywayo, informing him that the High Commissioner was now prepared to make known his decision on the boundary question, and desiring that Cetywayo should send envoys to the Tugela River, on a certain day in December, at a point not far from its mouth, to hear the decision and to settle other matters which were outstanding between the British Government and the Zulus,

The feeling throughout the colony, and, indeed, throughout all South Africa, was one of intense expectation. Black and white politicians waited with the greatest impatience the outcome of the meeting, which was fixed for the 11th of December.

Among the colonists there was but one feeling—that the Zulu question, which had been so long a bugbear to them, which had been so long a blight to their adopted land, might be now settled. They well knew it would not be child's play if there was war; and it was not likely that those of Dutch blood among them, who were old enough to remember the time when the war-cry of Dingaan's warriors rang through the land, and when their women and children were lying unburied below the Blaukrantz Hills, would think of joining in a Zulu war with a "light heart."

What the colonists wanted was not war, if it could possibly be avoided; what they did desire was that the unrest and uncertainty which had pervaded all classes of society in Natal, since Cetywayo's rule was shown to be an aggressive military despotism, should be put an end to, and that they should be as secure in Natal as in most parts of Her Majesty's dominions.

The natives of Natal were also keenly interested in the question, and were not at all confident of our capability to beat the Zulus, if war broke out Many of them had seen the Zulu king's power, but only knew ours by hearsay. The natives in Natal and to the eastward of the St. John's River had a vague notion of a great white Queen, who ruled by a piece of powerful and mysterious machinery called the Government, about which they would talk to each other with awe; but the evidences of the fighting powers of Government were not many compared to Cetywayo's thousands, "It is said you fight well," said an old Natal headman to a missionary, "and the Kafirs over there," continued he, nodding his head towards the Cape Colony, "say the red soldiers are very brave, but we have never seen you fight, and you won this country by coming and sitting down here."

"Poor fellows," a petty chief was heard to say while sitting on his haunches, with his headmen in a circle round him, watching a body of infantry pass his *kraal*, "how tired they must be of always marching! How their great Queen makes them walk!" When he was assured that they had only come a few miles that day, it appeared that he believed this (as he thought) unfortunate regiment was the same that he had seen two or three times pass his *kraal*, and that it was being marched round and round to keep order; and he could not for some time be made to believe the English had so many soldiers.

On the 11th of December, then, the Zulu envoys met the representatives of the British Government, and the High Commissioner's terms were duly communicated to them.

The communications consisted of two messages. The first message concerned the boundary award.

This message made known the award of the Boundary Commissioners, which had been confirmed by the High Commissioner. The award giving back to the Zulus, as it did, a large tract of land, was acknowledged, by even those most inclined to befriend the Zulus, to be a very favourable one from the Zulu point of view, and one which ought to satisfy them, were it not for a condition which was attached to it. When deciding upon the boundary question, the Boundary Commissioners rode rapidly over a portion only of the disputed territory, and they failed to discover to what extent this district was populated by the Boers. The number of Boers who were *bonâ-fide* farmers and not squatters was stated to be between twelve and fifteen.

It was discovered later that the number of Dutch farmers who had built dwelling-houses, planted orchards, and made a permanent settlement in the land was over eighty. What was to become of these people? Some of them had inherited their farms; some bought them; all believed they had a *bonâ-fide* title to them. Nor were they of that class of "*trek*" or wandering Boer, which has brought the white and black races into antagonism with each other in some parts of South Africa; but all, or almost all, were real farmers, who believed their farms belonged to them as much, and that they had come by them as fairly, as any Natal colonist or Cape farmer.

It will, perhaps, astonish some who read these lines that there were people in South Africa who expected that, as soon as the award was made known, these eighty families would be ordered off their farms, driven away from their homes and hearths to begin life over again where and how they could. Luckily for the character for justice of English rule in South Africa, this was not to be allowed.

It is decided that this land (ran in other words the award) belongs to Zulu Land; therefore the Zulu king shall rule over it, and all who live in it shall be his subjects. The farmers who now own farms on it shall, if they wish, remain, but they shall pay what taxes the Zulu king shall impose, and there shall be a white magistrate to keep them in order and arrange matters between them and the Zulu king.

This was the purport of the first message. The second was of greater importance, and with it lay the question of peace or war.

In this message the High Commissioner briefly stated the case of the British Government.

While wishing to live on terms of friendliness with the Zulu king, and to act up to its promises in supporting his rule, Cetywayo's behaviour to the British Government had been such as to bring about a most serious crisis between the Government and the Zulu nation.

Cetywayo had been placed on the throne by the British Government on certain conditions. The principal of the conditions was, that the wholesale killing of his subjects should cease. This Cetywayo had agreed to, yet killing was now carried to a greater extent than ever before, and the land ran with blood.

But this was not all. Two of the sons of one of the important chiefs invaded British territory with an armed party, and dragged away from a *kraal*, in which she had taken refuge, a Zulu woman. Reparation for this offence against the British Government had been repeatedly demanded, but beyond a sum of £80 offered, no attempt had been made by the Zulu king to comply with the demands of the British Government. It was demanded that the men be given up to trial, and that a fine of five hundred head of cattle be paid for the outrage and the long delay in complying with the British Government's demands.

Again, two British subjects were, when on the banks of the Tugela River, in the month of September, 1878, seized by an armed party of Zulus, and not permitted to leave for some hours. This was an offence against the persons of two of the Queen's subjects which could not be passed over, and a fine of one hundred head of cattle must be paid for this offence.

Besides these two cases of complaint, there were the depredations and murders committed by the robber chief Umbelini on Transvaal territory. Umbelini must be seized and given up, to answer before the Transvaal law courts, for all the murders and robberies he had committed.

These three demands were easy for Cetywayo to comply with, and twenty days were given him for their fulfilment.

There was another part of the message which pointed out the state of things in Zulu Land, laying stress on the continual killing; on the keeping up of the large army, which was totally unnecessary, except for aggressive purposes; on the men being prevented marrying and settling down, and the people being therefore continually kept in an unsettled state, and becoming more and more eager for war and less inclined to live peaceably. It was demanded that the military system should be abolished, and men should not be forced to become soldiers, except in defence of their country; that all men should be allowed to marry when they would; and that all Zulus should have a fair trial, and not be killed without a hearing.

Also, in order that misunderstandings should not arise between the Government and the Zulu nation, an officer of the Queen should (as Cetywayo had formerly often asked) be sent to him, who should be the instrument of the Government, and be the means of communication between the Government and the Zulu king.

As these conditions entailed consultation with the chiefs of the Zulu nation (who were, however, at this time assembled at the king's *kraal*), thirty days was fixed as the time within which these terms were to be accepted.

These were to be the last words of the British Government.

Thus, after half a year's *parleying*; after demanding for six months, in most moderate terms, redress for an outrage which in Europe would have been atoned for in a week, or would have been followed by a declaration of war, Her Majesty's representative ventured to give a barbarian ruler (who, though placed on his throne by Her Majesty's Government, had been for years past a menace to the colony of Natal) the option, once and for all, of complying with the demands of Government, or of standing the consequences.

After the 11th of December, matters were placed in the hands of the military authorities, and we must turn and see what the military situation was.

For the past six months all the attention of the military authorities in South Africa had been engrossed by the unprotected state of Natal, and the work of defence and of preparing for a possible Zulu war had been going on. Pressing application had been made to England early in the year for more troops, but the public interest (soon to be so terribly awakened) was as yet feeble in South African matters, and with affairs in Europe looking so threatening, and with a possible war on our Indian frontier, it was not thought expedient to spare the number or the description of troops which were demanded.

Two battalions of infantry were, however, sent out, and were a very welcome addition to the strength of infantry at the disposal of the general commanding.

Roughly, the force at the disposal of the general commanding was as follows:—Guns, 20; cavalry and mounted infantry, 1200; infantry, 6000; natives, 9000. It must be remembered, in calculating the force available for the invasion of Zulu Land, a considerable reduction—about a sixth—must be made in the numbers of the infantry, to allow for garrisons and detachments to hold the line of communications.

It had been proposed, some months before the delivery of the message of the High Commissioner to the Zulu envoys in December, to commence enrolling, organizing, and disciplining a native force. But this course of action was not approved by the Natal Government, lest it should aggravate the Zulu king and bring matters to a crisis. This might or might not have been the case, but the result of not commencing the organization of a native force sooner was that a large proportion of the native troops were undisciplined, untrained, and not to be depended upon.

The mounted natives, of which there were about twelve hundred, were mostly of Basuto extraction and worked admirably, and were a very valuable addition to our forces; but it was otherwise with the native infantry. These were chiefly of Zulu extraction. Some, indeed, may have only escaped from Zulu Land a few months before they came to serve against their late much-dreaded ruler, and the same man who, in a Zulu regiment, would rush madly forward to within a few yards of the muzzle of the breech-loader and command the admiration of his white enemy, would, fighting in our ranks, be represented by a spiritless native, during the course of an action squatting on his haunches and firing off his rifle in the air, only useful to race after a beaten foe.

We have all seen the difference between the country lout who slouches away from the farmyard to take the shilling in the nearest country town, and the upright soldier who returns to the village a couple of years afterwards, his mind improved no less than his body.

This transformation is just the converse of what took place in the Zulu brave, who, emancipated from the iron discipline of Cetywayo's army, relapsed into a harmless savage.

By dint of strict training and discipline, with confidence in their officers, and accustomed to be led by them, the Natal natives would become, doubtless, excellent soldiers; but they, like Cetywayo's men, require to be well disciplined, and the Natal Native Contingent of 1878 was no more to be compared to a Zulu regiment than a hastily armed battalion of French peasants of 1870 with a regiment of the Prussian line.

The force intended to act against the Zulu king was divided into three columns, which were to move into Zulu Land on three lines of advance, keeping up intercommunication as far as possible, and which were to effect a junction in the neighbourhood of the king's *kraal*.

The three columns were commanded, taking them in order from the right advance near the Sea, by Brigadier-General Pearson, Colonel Glyn, and Brigadier-General Wood. There were also two smaller and subsidiary columns under Colonels Rowlands and Durnford, which were to join the main columns when they had commenced their advance.

The map of Zulu Land and Natal has, since the beginning of 1879, been so carefully studied that it is almost needless to mention that the Tugela and Buffalo rivers form the boundary between Natal and Zulu Land. It was intended that General Pearson's column should invade Zulu Land at the Lower Drift, a ford not far from the sea; that Colonel Glyn's should enter the country from Rorke's Drift, and General Wood's from the north-west from the position in which he was encamped in the Utrecht district.

The great difficulty in preparing efficiently for the campaign was the difficulty of transport.

In England it is hard for us to realize what the now well-known phrase "difficulty of transport" means; but let anyone in a hurry to go inland disembark at Natal, and he will soon understand the matter. He probably has what seems to him a very moderate amount of baggage, which he manages to get on shore in a day or two, and goes his way rejoicing, to make arrangements to depart to his destination (which is, say, a hundred miles off) the first thing the next day. He finds that all the places are taken in the public post-carts for the next three days, and that only fourteen pounds of luggage may be carried by each passenger; that, as regards his baggage, there is no room on any waggon for some days; and that he will be a lucky man if his possessions reach their destination in a fortnight. This is difficulty of transport to an individual, discomfort and delay; to an army it may mean starvation and ruin.

The army in Natal had to be supplied with breadstuffs, clothing material—with everything, in fact, but meat—almost entirely from the sea. The moment the stores were landed at the sea base, Durban, difficulties began. They had to be brought on waggons, sometimes drawn by mules, but commonly by oxen, to the various *depôts*, or despatched in some cases direct to the several columns. It was, of course, necessary that all the *depôts* should be full of food before the advance began, and that each column should be self-supporting for a certain number of days.

An ox waggon can carry, say, six thousand pounds of biscuit, or six days' biscuit ration for one thousand men, who are lying one hundred and fifty miles from the sea-coast, whence the biscuit has to come. An ox waggon travels on an average fifteen miles a day under favourable circumstances. How many waggons would be needed to keep the thousand men supplied with biscuit?

This calculation will perhaps enable some idea to be formed of the time and number of waggons which were required to place two months' supplies on the line of the Tugela for the force to be employed in Zulu Land.

The twenty days wore rapidly away amid general speculation and surmise as to the course the Zulu king would pursue.

Would he accept the award and refuse the other terms? Would he ask for more time, and send excuses as before? Would he send in Sirayo's sons, promise to catch Umbelini, offer a ready acceptance to the other terms, and put off compliance with them until he had persuaded the Government to send the troops out of the country?

The course pursued by Cetywayo was a very fair sample of native diplomacy.

He first delayed sending any answer at all. Then he sent various unofficial and vague messages to several border agents, by men of inferior rank, to say "that he would give up the sons of Sirayo, but wanted more time"; "that he would not give up the sons of Sirayo, but would pay more cattle for them"; "that he would consider the messages with his council, but must have more time."

The Zulu king, however, sent no formal message to the High Commissioner or Lieutenant-Governor, as Zulu custom and etiquette demanded, and as he would have been very careful to do had he wished to place matters on a friendly basis. As to the boundary award (although its advantages to the Zulus must have taken him by surprise), he ignored it altogether.

The news which could be obtained at this time from Zulu Land was somewhat meagre.

It was evident from the reports received that older men among the king's counsellors were urging him to keep friends with the white man, and that those few who knew the terms demanded by the British Government were urging him to comply with them. The young regiments were, however, eager to fight, and clamorous to be led against the "*amasoja.*"

The king himself, after he had heard of the small size of our columns, expressed himself as confident of being able "to eat them up one after the other." He sent orders to some of his *indunas* on the Transvaal border, who were collecting some cattle which had been raided from the farmers, to return them to the Zulus who had carried them off, as he meant to fight; and, last but not least, he called up his army without ornaments or badges, *i.e.*, in fighting order, to the grand *kraal.*

★★★★★★

It is curious to turn back to the opinions of the Dutchmen in Natal at this time, and to find how accurately they foretold what would happen. The Dutch Boers, it must be remembered, were the people who had seen the Zulus fight. The English never had; but the old "*foretrekkers*" in what is now Transvaal territory, and on the borders of Basuto Land, no less than in Natal and Zulu Land, had often met the warriors of Dingaan, and had been taught by them many a bloody lesson before they learned to adopt tactics to baffle their savage and cunning enemy.

"Cetywayo means to fight you," said an old Dutchman, himself one of those who had *laagered* their waggons in Zulu Land thirty years before, but who was still stalwart and upright; "he means to fight you. The Zulus have had time to forget the good lessons we taught them when Dingaan was king, and they think their guns have made them equal to *you*. But I hope the English soldiers will beware; they are fighting now a different foe from the Cape Colony Kafir. Ah, yes; the Zulus are different. I much fear the '*Rooi-laatjes*' (red-jackets) have been fighting the Gaikas and Galekas so long that they will undervalue the Zulu."

CHAPTER 7

Preparations

At this juncture the conviction among many in England seems to have been that the war was precipitated, and the campaign opened with unnecessary haste; that a few months' delay, to afford time for more troops (if any chanced to be on their way) to arrive, would have done no harm—more, would have been the proper course to pursue, taking into consideration the European and Indian complications which were embarrassing the Government at the time.

The war, perhaps inevitable, was at the moment very inopportune (people reasoned). There were great matters under consideration involving questions of vast importance to the empire at large. Why should a petty barbarian monarch be allowed to embarrass the British empire at such a time? Granted war was inevitable, surely a few months' delay could have been easily arranged?

This would have been, perhaps, sound argument if brought forward in 1875, or even 1876 or 1877, or if the Zulu question had just become formidable. But it must not be forgotten that the Zulu difficulty, which only attracted the full attention of the English nation after Isandhlwana, and which seemed to many a new complication, and therefore one which could have been easily staved off, was really a difficulty whose solution had caused great anxiety for four years past, and whose peaceable settlement had become, during the last two years or eighteen months, almost impossible.

It was easy for able writers in England to talk of the obvious facility with which a Zulu campaign might have been put off to a more fitting period, and of the reckless haste with which "this war of aggression" was hurried on, and to point to the long peace in Panda's time as a proof of the pacific inclinations of the Zulu king and people. But their words, convincing as they might seem to English readers, would have conveyed no sort of comfort to the nearly ruined Transvaal Boers, and to the sturdy though disheartened German emigrants, who were huddled together for protection round the little hamlets of Utrecht and Luneberg, wondering how long their provisions would hold out, if they were not soon enabled to break *laager* and go back to their homes to cultivate their land; nor would such opinions have reassured the Natal farmer, living on the banks of the Buffalo or Tugela River, who had known what a Zulu *impi* could and had done in the way of invasion, and had received news of the Zulu king's probable intentions from the trader hurrying out of Zulu Land with stock half sold off, himself acting on friendly warning from some of Cetywayo's petty chiefs.

The fixed opinion amongst the ablest and most experienced of those skilled in Zulu strategy and politics, as to the intention of the Zulu king, was as follows:—

Cetywayo would gather his harvest and complete his preparations, and then, when the Tugela (in the early part of the year flooded, and a dangerous obstacle to a barbarian army) had sunk in its bed, he would commence hostilities, either by small raiding parties, or, following the example of his forefathers Chaka and Dingaan, he would throw one *impi* into Natal (as he entreated Sir Theophilus Shepstone to allow him to do two years before) and send another to eat up the farmers on the Transvaal border.

And what would have been the result if Cetywayo had been given an opportunity of carrying out such a course of action? After the experience of the Zulu war, of Isandhlwana and of Intombi, it does not require a strong imagination to picture the simultaneous inroad of two or three cattle-raiding Zulu *impis*, avoiding our fortified positions, advancing through the country, sacking homesteads and hamlets, killing man, woman, and child, collecting cattle and booty, and reaching the Zulu bank of the Tugela or Buffalo before it was well known in the colony what was happening.

One can imagine the harassed soldiers; the natives, first terrified, then lukewarm, then treacherous; the panic-stricken colonists; the Transvaal Boers, in open revolt at seeing no chance of gaining a hearing for their complaints; and, last but not least, the news that there was war flying through the land to every *kraal* (in the mysterious way news does travel among the black races in South Africa), giving heart to every chief who had a grudge, real or imaginary, against Government: "the great king had begun to wash his *assegais*, and had invaded Natal, and intended to drive the white man into the sea." We should have to turn to the Indian Mutiny for a fit comparison for such a situation.

And in what temper would the English people have been then? Enraged and cut to the quick as they were by the loss of a British regiment, of British colours, and of British guns, by the loss of brave men who had died in hopeless yet open fight, how would the English nation have received the news of massacres of farmers and their wives and children, of the laying waste of one British colony which had been crying warnings to the mother country for years past, of the laying waste of another which we had taken possession of in order to protect its white inhabitants from the very danger which had now been suffered to sweep over it? To whom would they have turned as responsible for this, but to the tried servant of Queen and country, for whom words have not been strong enough to express his wrongdoing in endeavouring to protect those placed in his charge?

What did happen was bad enough. But Evelyn Wood covered the Transvaal; and with his column and with General Pearson's on their flanks and rear, and a river liable to heavy floods, which might affect their retreat, the Zulus did not fancy the undertaking, and preferred, after Isandhlwana, to continue their harvesting, and to wait to eat up the white soldiers at leisure, in place of invading Natal under such conditions. The disaster at Isandhlwana was a terrible blow, but the moral advantage of the attack still was left with us. We were still in the country, and the Natal natives pointed to Kambula Hill and Ekowe as a proof that we were not going to be eaten up, but were only waiting till the great white Queen should send some more soldiers out of the sea, before we again continued our way towards the Zulu king's *kraal*.

The above may be regarded as the diplomatic or political reasons for the necessity of commencing the Zulu campaign early in 1879 5 what may be termed the military considerations all urged an early campaign no less strongly.

Delay in the outbreak of hostilities would have been of such obvious advantage to the Zulu king, that it was only the overwhelming confidence he had in his capability for eating up the English forces that could have prevented him attempting to gain time by the ruses which are the very A B C of Zulu diplomacy.

By the beginning of the new year, 1879, the British troops were nearly ready; the Zulu army was not. Our commissariat arrangements were on the point of being completed; theirs had not begun. In other words, the Zulus had not been able to commence getting in their harvest, for the *mealies*, which form their staple food, would not be ready for picking for another two months at least.

Again, the white population of Natal, men, women, and children, was under twenty thousand; the black population was over three hundred and fifty thousand. The feelings of a large number of the latter were not accurately known, and though the attitude of the chiefs and headmen was generally satisfactory, the bulk of the native population of Natal could not be depended upon to afford anything more than passive support, and that only so long as they were pretty secure in their own *kraals*. It was all-important, as has been remarked, that the terrain of operations should be in Zulu Land, and not in Natal, and also that we should gain the moral advantages to be drawn from making the first attack.

There were two other reasons, each of them important ones. The first has been already touched upon.

The Buffalo and the Tugela Rivers, which in the months of January, February, and March are sometimes in full and rapid flood, almost always unfordable, and therefore a formidable barrier to the invasion of Natal by a Zulu *impi*, become in the later months of the year streams of water of insignificant volume, and consequently very generally fordable.

If the invasion of Zulu Land were to take place at the commencement of the year, her river barrier would form, as it were, a second line of defence for Natal, in case the Zulu force should attempt to evade the advance of our attacking columns.

The last reason was that, in the beginning of May, the grass on which the waggon oxen and the horses of the mounted men would depend is dry enough to burn, and would be burnt by the Zulus, and the difficulties of moving troops would thus be a hundred-fold increased, were we not to finish the campaign before the end of this month. As it actually occurred, there was grass until long after the ordinary time, as the rains came many weeks later than is usual in this part of South Africa.

Besides Natal, it must not be forgotten, there was the Transvaal also to be protected, and a general advance from the line of the Blood, Buffalo, and Tugela rivers would attain this object, and cover the southeast boundary of the Transvaal.

CHAPTER 8

The Spears Are Washed

This then was the situation on New Year's Day, 1879, at the expiration of the twenty days, the time named for the compliance with the demands which only required the king's sanction. Three main columns were in position on the Lower Tugela, Rorke's Drift on the Buffalo, and at Bemta's Kop near the Blood River; column composed of natives, under Colonel Durnford, which was intended afterwards to be merged with No. 3, or Colonel Glyn's column, was watching Middle Drift on the Tugela; and a small column under Colonel Rowlands was marching from the Transvaal, on the north-west boundary of Zulu Land, to join hands with No. 4, or Brigadier-General Wood's column.

The advance, as has already been pointed out, was to be made by three main columns.

These three columns were to advance into Zulu Land at the expiration of the thirty days, and each to firmly establish an advanced *depôt* at some good defensible position, where wood and water would be easily procurable.

The aim of the right column. No. 1, or General Pearson's, was the mission station at Ekowe. No. 2 Column was to remain slightly in rear of the advance, to defend the Natal border; No. 3 Column was to form its advanced *depôt* somewhere in the neighbourhood of the Ibabamango Mountain; and No. 4 Column was in like manner to advance over the Blood River to a good position for forming a temporary base.

Zulu Land was at this time so little known, and reliable data regarding it so hard to procure, that it was intended to leave much to the column commanders.

The general idea in moving forward from the advanced *depôts* was to advance on Ulundi (each column opening communications with the others as soon as practicable), and to concentrate as soon as the nature of the country would permit.

The Zulu Land army was assembling at the king's *kraal*, where the king had also summoned all the headmen and chiefs of the nation.

The king did not suffer the chiefs and headmen to leave his *kraal*, except to take parts in the different expeditions against the British forces during the time the war lasted. This prevented any intriguing or intercourse with the enemy on their part, and also prevented the Zulu people learning the real state of the case as regards the causes of the war, and enabled the stories which the king spread throughout Zulu Land (that the white men would take the Zulu people's land and drive them out of the country) to pass uncontradicted and to gain credence.

Some ten miles below the junction of the Blood and Buffalo rivers is Rorke's Drift, on the latter river. The valley of the Buffalo above Rorke's Drift is open, closing with rocky hills and *kloofs* immediately below it.

On the Zulu or north bank of the river, above the drift, the ground is open for some little distance, but on the Natal or southern bank the hills trend in towards the bank in a slanting direction, meeting the river just below the drift, so that there is a high hill just overlooking the shallows. This hill, however, is only partly joined to the range of hills which form the Natal side of the valley, and stands somewhat by itself, and in the gap thus formed stood the Swedish Mission station, screened by this hill from the river.

Some four hundred yards away from this house, on some level ground above the river side, the camp of No. 3 Column was pitched on the evening of the 9th of January, the last day but one of the thirty days.

The twenty days, the time allowed for the surrender of Sirayo's sons, expired on the 31st of December, but in order that every opportunity might be afforded the Zulu king, should he desire to treat, no movement of troops into Zulu Land was to take place until the end of the thirty days, the period fixed for the full compliance with all our demands.

The 10th of January was spent by No. 3 busily enough, in completing the loading of the provision waggons and in finishing the two ponts which were to take the infantry guns and waggons across the river. The day passed, and neither at the Lower Tugela, Rorke's Drift, nor at Bemta's Kop (the headquarters of the three columns) were any signs received of either Cetywayo's compliance with our demands or even of his willingness to treat.

No. 3 Column consisted of Harness's battery of Royal Artillery, a squadron of mounted infantry, a squadron of Natal mounted police, and three Natal volunteer corps; the mounted corps numbering together, about three hundred and fifty men. The British infantry were represented by the first and second battalions of the 24th, together numbering about a thousand bayonets; the first battalion being three companies, the second battalion one company short. There were also two battalions of Natal Native Contingent, numbering over two thousand men, and there were about a hundred waggons belonging to the columns, carrying tents, supplies, and ammunition.

At daybreak on the 10th of January the crossing of the Tugela commenced. The mounted men crossed at the shallows, the 1-24th on the two ponts, and one battalion of the Native Contingent at a ford a quarter of a mile upstream. The 2-24th were lining the ridge above the ponts, and Harness's guns were in battery in a position above the shallows under the hill, which enabled them to enfilade the Zulu bank of the river. As soon as the cavalry and 24th were well across and had crowned the ridge on the Zulu side, the remainder of the force followed, and then the waggons.

This was weary work. Each ponderous waggon had to be brought down as near the pont as possible, then the oxen outspanned and driven round to the shallows to wade and swim across, while the waggon was passed on to the pont by hand. As I was seeing this done, three Dutch Boers came down to the river's side and asked if I could allow them to cross, as they wanted to ride to a point on the Blood River to meet General Wood.

They were evidently well-to-do men. They rode good horses; each had a good rifle and an armed "after-rider" with a spare horse. One ranged his horse up alongside mine, and while waiting for the pont to return, began pointing out some of the landmarks in the neighbourhood.

"See, *kaptein*," said he in his Dutch accent, "see that *kop* to the north, round and grassy, with no trees; it is the Doom Berg, and fine grazing there be round it. There is Sirayo's *kraal*," continued he, turning more to the east, "under those red rocks; and see yon more to the right, that pointed *kop*. That, I think, the Zulus call Isandhlwana."

By nightfall nearly all the waggons had been got across the river, and all the troops (except the B company of the second battalion 24th, who were to garrison Rorke's Drift, and who were bemoaning their sad fate at being obliged to stay behind where they should miss all the fighting) were encamped on Zulu soil. The cavalry of the force had, after crossing, swept round the country and had communicated with General Wood's column. Very few Zulus were to be seen, and the promise of the Zulu king that we should be attacked before the water of the Tugela had dried on our feet seemed as if it would not be kept.

It was found, however, that Sirayo's people were holding their *kraal*, which was in a strong position about four miles from the river, by the Ingutu Hill, and it was decided to dislodge, them.

On the morning of the 12th of January portions of the first and second 24th, a battalion of the Contingent, and the mounted men, left camp shortly after daybreak.

An hour and a half's marching brought the force into the valley of the Bashee Spruit, a little stream running past the Ingutu Mountain into the Buffalo.

The Ingutu Mountain lay north-north-east and south-south-east, and, like many hills in Zulu Land, became almost inaccessible within sixty feet of the summit, the inaccessible part being pierced with holes and caves.

On crossing the Bashee stream, and on ascending the valley on the other side, Zulus began to be visible hovering about the rocky recesses of the hill, and the war-cry began to sound through the *kloofs*.

The force here separated—the infantry moving to attack the west side, and the cavalry being sent to turn the position from the eastward, where the country was more open and suitable for mounted men.

As the Zulus saw the mounted men moving away as it were, they began to taunt us, making their voices sound through the still morning air in the curious way natives can: "What were we doing riding along down there?" "We had better try and come up"; "Were we looking for a place to build our *kraals*?" etc., etc. This badinage, which was accompanied by a few shots by way of emphasis, did not last long; for arriving at a good position for protecting the horses, half the force dismounted and attacked the hill, and in about an hour had driven the enemy out of the hill and across the valley on the other side. One of the first men shot was one of Sirayo's sons.

While the cavalry were charging the hill from the east, the infantry had done the same from the west.

By nine o'clock the fighting was over. Our loss was two natives killed; one officer, one non-commissioned officer, and twelve natives wounded. The Zulu loss was about forty killed.

This was the first engagement of the Zulu war, and it greatly enraged the Zulu king, who, immediately on receiving the news of the destruction of the *kraal* of one of his favourite captains, gave orders for the formation of the forces which were to eat up the English columns.

According to custom, the king reviewed them before they left, so that they might hear his last words—

> I am sending you against the white man, the white man who has invaded Zulu Land and driven away our cattle. You are to go against the column at the Ishyane [Rorke's Drift], and drive it back into Natal; and if the river will allow, follow it into Natal, and go on up to the Drakensberg.

Such, according to a man of the Nokenke Regiment, were the orders of the king to the main body of his army.

For the next week the whole energies of the column were absorbed in endeavouring to make the old waggon track, along which we were to advance, passable. Parts of the road were hard, and, if care was taken not to drive the waggons recklessly against rocks and boulders, were passable enough; but there were low-lying bits of the track on soft soil, made swampy by springs and wet weather, into which the heavy waggons sank axle-deep.

By the 19th of January the road was reported passable. The column accordingly, striking camp at daybreak next morning, marched in a south-easterly direction from Rorke's Drift, and Monday night, the 20th of January, saw the force encamped under Isandhlwana Hill.

Two days before, on the 17th, the Zulu king had despatched his forces from the grand *kraal* in three divisions, against the three columns. The smallest was sent against the Dutchman's column (General Wood's); the mass of his troops, between fifteen and twenty thousand, against "Somtseu's" column (No. 3 Column); and about five or six thousand against the Englishman's, or General Pearson's column.

The Zulus thus named the three columns. General Wood had a force of Dutch *burghers* with him, so No. 4 Column was distinguished as the Dutchman's column; Sir Theophilus Shepstone had paid a visit to Lord Chelmsford at his camp, and was still imagined by the Zulus to be at the general's headquarters; and General Pearson's force was called the Englishman's column.

Besides the Zulu troops composing these three *impis*, the Zula king retained a strong force with him, as he expected an attack from the direction of Delagoa Bay, whence many rumours had reached him of the ships we had sent down there, and of our intentions to attack him through the Amatonga country.

The Isandhlwana camp fronted nearly east, and was partly pitched on a neck between two small hills, the hill on the left or north being the higher and being inaccessible, and partly on the slopes below this inaccessible hill. This hill gives its name to the position, and is joined on its side remote from the neck by a range of low rocky hills, which curve round to the left and left front of the position. The hill on the right or south trends away in a more or less direct line, south from the position.

The front of the position is open ground, but broken by *sluits*, watercourses, and "*dongas*."

To the rear of the position the ground sinks steeply to a little stream falling into the Buffalo. Down this incline, crossing the stream, winds the waggon road to Rorke' Drift. The crow's flight, however, to the river would be to the right rear of the position, nearly following the course of the little stream above mentioned.

On the morning of the 21st, a force of mounted men under Major Dartnell, and of Native Contingent under Commandant Lonsdale, was despatched to examine the country surrounding the *kraal* of Matyan, a chief whose stronghold, some ten miles away from Isandhlwana Hill, was supposed to be of importance. Late in the day it was decided that, instead of returning to camp that night, this force should bivouac in the vicinity of Matyan's *kraal*. Though the object of the reconnaissance was to obtain information to guide the operations of the main column, there does not appear to have been any advantage to gain by the force not returning to camp, as a set-off against the risk of its being attacked by the enemy and overwhelmed before assistance could arrive.

The force bivouacking near Matyan's *kraal* passed an uneasy night. The two native battalions were restless and scared. There were Zulus all around them, they said, and they felt they were a long way from the white soldiers.

The enemy was doubtless in the neighbourhood, and an express was about midnight despatched to the Isandhlwana camp to ask for support, and to report that an attack was expected at daybreak.

The messenger reached camp at about 2.30 a.m. on the morning of the 22nd of January, and orders were then given for a force consisting of four guns, the mounted men, the second battalion 24th Regiment, and a corps of Native Pioneers, to march at daybreak to effect a junction with the force near Matyan's *kraal*.

On looking back to that Wednesday morning, how every little detail seems to stand out in relief! The hurried and careless farewell to the comrade in my tent, whose name will not be forgotten while the Zulu war is remembered; my servant, who was to leave for Natal that very morning, saying when he brought my horse, "I shall be here, sir, when you come back; the waggons are not to start today, now this force is going out"; the half-laughing condolences to the 1-24th as they watched the troops move out of camp; the men not for duty turning out for the routine work of the camp; the position of the tents and of the waggons—many trifles fixed in the mind serve to make stronger the contrast between the departure and the return to that ill-fated camp.

At half-past four the force already alluded to marched out of camp in a south-easterly direction. It was barely light when we left the camp, but in a short time the conical hill in the direction of which we had to march became visible. The track was fairly good, but here and there was crossed by the *dongas*, or sandy ravines, which are so common in Zulu Land. They are formed by the watershed from the hills, and they commence as little watercourses in the hillside, becoming much wider and broader as they reach the valley or the plain. Some are so large that they can conceal a large number of men, and in a *donga* country scouting has to be very carefully and thoroughly performed. The sides of some of these *dongas* had to be cut away to get the guns down. But we were not delayed long by this, as the company of Native Pioneers were kept well up with the advance-guard, and were hurried to the front when the scouts reported an impracticable *donga*, and almost as soon as the guns came up the men had scraped, picked, and pushed away enough of the side to enable Harness's 7-pounders to make their way down with the aid of drag-ropes.

The sun came up above the hills to the right front of our trench, and the morning became very hot, the sky perfectly clear, and only the faintest breath of wind. The men, however, pushed merrily on in high spirits, hoping that at last they were going to have "a real bit of fighting."

At 8.30 a.m. we arrived underneath the conical hill, and found near it the force which had been detached the previous day. An advance was at once ordered in the direction the Zulu force was reported to be, but the morning was spent in endeavouring to get to close quarters with an enemy who could and did avoid us at pleasure.

The cavalry of the force exchanged long shots at a body of Zulus who retreated and dispersed among the hills. The Native Contingent and a detachment of the infantry cut off a small body of Zulus, and forced them to take refuge in some caves, whence they were driven with a loss of about thirty or forty killed.

Shortly after noon the hills among which we were operating were clear of the enemy, and the men were ordered to get their dinners. It was a welcome order, for the infantry, having started from camp at 4.30 a.m., had marched for four hours, and had been toiling up and down the hills under the hot South African sun ever since.

About 1 p.m. it was decided that the camp at Isandhlwana should be struck, and the headquarters advanced to a position selected near the conical hill. The troops at Isandhlwana were to march on the morning of the 23rd to the camp near the conical hill, and the troops already in the neighbourhood were to bivouac on the new camping-ground that night.

Lord Chelmsford and the headquarters staff, after these orders had been issued, started with the mounted men to return to the Isandhlwana camp.

At 3 p.m. we marched to the site of the new camp. We had just off-saddled, and many of us were half asleep, thinking, as is usually the case with men living in the open air, of when we should get our next meal. Suddenly (it was about half-past three) someone said, "Hallo! there's a man in a hurry. He ought to have a horse behind every hill if he intends to keep on at that rate."

"Who's the man?" said another.

"I can't see; have you your glasses?" said the first speaker. "By Jove! it's G——" (naming one of the general's *aides-de-camp*). "I hope nothing has gone wrong." Interest in the rider being awakened, we watched him gallop on up the hill towards us, his horse evidently blown and weary. "Well, G——, what is it? you seem in a great hurry."

"The General's orders are that you are to saddle up and march on Isandhlwana at once," said G——; "the Zulus have got into our camp."

"The Zulus have! You're not joking?"

"I wish I was. Lonsdale met the General about five miles from the camp; he had ridden up close to the camp, and had seen the enemy in amongst the tents. The General is waiting for you with the mounted men."

"Boot and saddle" sounded, and in a quarter of an hour the force was on its march back. While on the way we tried hard to solve satisfactorily the problem—"The Zulus in our camp, what had become of the force left to hold it?"

Half an hour after we had left our temporary bivouac, Isandhlwana Hill came in sight, and with field-glasses we could see the tents still standing. Surely there could not have been a serious attack threatening, or the tents would have been struck at once.

On the march we met two or three Natal Native Pioneers who had been left behind, and who had 'started late to join their company, and had bidden when the Zulus advanced. These men were closely questioned as we hurried along. "They had seen," they said, "the hills and all the ground near the camp thick with Zulus; they had attacked the camp; there had been much firing; the big guns had fired, oh, many times; the Zulus had got very near the camp, but they could not say if they had got into it." On the whole the matter seemed so improbable, so impossible, that we began to think there must have been exaggeration somewhere, and to hope things might not be so bad after all. "There had been an attack on the camp, perhaps a severe one. At the worst the Zulus had got near the camp and had been beaten, and were waiting to resume their onset. We should reach in time to take the enemy in flank and rear, if daylight would only hold out"

Though the men of the 24th, weary as they were, stepped out well, the road seemed a hundred times longer than when we had stepped it twelve hours before, and it was half-past seven before we met the general, whom we found awaiting us at a point two and a half miles from Isandhlwana. Then our new-formed hopes were swept away, and we learnt that the worst news we had heard was only too true, and there was no doubt but that a great disaster had befallen our arms.

The Zulus had taken our camp, and we were in Zulu Land at that moment without ammunition or provisions, and we must regain at all hazards the road to Rorke's Drift that night

The general said a few words of encouragement to the men, and was answered by a cheer, and then the force was formed up to advance on the ridge of Isandhlwana.

The four guns of Harness's battery were formed in line on the road; on either flank of the guns were three companies of the 2-24th, and next again a battalion of the Natal Contingent; on the flanks were the mounted men.

It fell quite dark as we neared the camp, and we could see fires burning near the ridge, where we expected to find the enemy holding it in force. At about two thousand yards the line was halted, while the guns opened and fired two rounds. We advanced to within about twelve hundred yards, and fired two more rounds. Then, with fixed bayonets, we advanced into the camp, and made our way through, men and horses stumbling and falling over tents half-upset, broken waggons, dead bodies of soldiers and of Zulus, dead oxen, dead horses, dead mules, burst sacks of grain, empty ammunition boxes, articles of camp equipment; and on the ridge, amongst the dead bodies of our comrades, formed our bivouac.

And what had happened at Isandhlwana camp since we left it that morning?

When the force to attack Matyan moved out of camp on the morning of the 22nd, the Zulu army, some twenty thousand strong, under command of Umnyamana, was lying still in its bivouac in the valley of the 'Nguto range.

The force here collected consisted of the *élite* of the Zulu army, and included the king's body guard, the Undi corps, numbering nearly ten thousand men. The Tulwana, the king's special regiment, and the Nkobamakosi (or "the ring-benders") were the two crack regiments of the Undi corps. These two were so jealous of each other that they had to be separated as much as possible to prevent fights occurring. It was not long ago that a serious fracas, resulting in many deaths, had taken place between the two regiments, on account of each regiment claiming the right to march first out of the king's *kraal*.

There were also the Nokenke, or "the dividers," and the Umhlanga, or "the rushes"—young regiments drafted on to an old corps of Chaka's, which had all but disappeared, being represented only by a few old men of seventy-eight or eighty years of age.

Then the Umcityu corps, "the sharp-pointed ones"—so called because in a quarrel which took place between Cetywayo and one of his brothers, part of the corps took one side and part another, which caused it to be compared to a stick pointed at both ends; the Uve and the Umbonambi, "the evil-seers," and the Nodwengu corps, who all considered themselves among the best of the Zulu army.

The army then was lying still. No fires were allowed, lest they should betray to the white army the Zulu position.

No orders for an attack had been given, nor was it intended that an attack should be made that day, as it. was new moon—in Zulu parlance, "the moon was dead," and it was an unlucky day. The attack was intended to take place the next day, the 23rd of January.

However, a part of the Umcityu corps, while changing its position from some reason or another, was seen and fired on by the scouts of No. 3 Column. The Zulus returned the fire, and other Zulu regiments then rose and ran to the sound of the firing, in no order or organization.

Discipline, however, was soon restored, and about 10 a.m. an organized attack on the position, according to Zulu tactics, was commenced. The Zulu front was, however, not parallel to ours, but the attack of their main body was directed on our left front.

The whole army moved round to the left front of the English position, sending out two horns, or flank attacks. These horns, continually lengthening, are supplied with men from the rear of the main body or chest of the army, which keeps up a steady and slow advance, until one or both of the horns have made good their ground, when the chest charges to overwhelm the enemy.

The force left in camp on the 22nd was as follows:—Royal Artillery, 2 guns, 1 officer, and 65 non-commissioned officers and men; 5 companies first battalion 24th—16 officers and 350 non-commissioned officers and men; one company second battalion 24th—5 officers and about 80 men. There were 26 men of the Natal police, 4 officers and 32 men of the Natal volunteers, about 70 officers and non-commissioned officers of the Natal Contingent, and 350 natives. Besides this, there were over a hundred camp followers, bandsmen, servants, clerks, cooks, etc., etc.

This force was considered sufficient for the defence of the camp, especially as it would in a few hours be reinforced by Colonel Durnford with two hundred and fifty mounted natives and a rocket battery.

After the departure of the force to attack Matyan, the ordinary routine of the camp went on as usual. Picquets were relieved, *videttes* posted, road parties sent out of camp, oxen driven off to feed.

At six o'clock the *videttes* on the left of the camp reported parties of the enemy in sight. These, however, either retired, or more probably concealed themselves in the folds of the ground.

At eight o'clock, however, numerous bodies of the enemy were reported on the left and left front, and as an attack appeared imminent, the road parties were recalled and the men stood to their arms.

At 9.30 a.m., or shortly after. Colonel Durnford with his mounted men arrived in camp, and as senior officer took over the command from Colonel Pulleine.

For some time past, different reports regarding the enemy's movements were reported by the *videttes* and scouts, and shortly after ten a report arrived that the enemy was retiring in all directions, making off towards Matyan's stronghold, apparently with the intention of reinforcing the *impi* which was supposed to be engaged with the general.

To prevent this, Colonel Durnford took two troops of his Basutos, with the rocket battery, and advanced at a gallop, sending two troops, under Captain George Shepstone, over the hills to the left front.

The situation at about 10.30 was as follows:—

The 24th was standing in column near the centre of the camp, except two companies on picquet, which were near the *donga* which ran round the bottom slope of the camp, about six hundred yards from Isandhlwana Hill.

The guns were in position on the left of the infantry.

The native infantry were on the hill to the left of the camp.

Two troops of mounted Basutos, and the rocket battery, with a company of native infantry as escort, had advanced rapidly from the camp. The rocket battery, marching much more slowly than the mounted men, soon fell behind, and was suddenly, about eleven o'clock, attacked in flank by a body of Zulus, and cut to pieces three miles from camp.

Captain George Shepstone was engaging the enemy over the hills on the left front.

The waggons were inspanned.

Colonel Durnford, having advanced about five miles from camp, seems to have come upon the chest or main body of the Zulu army. He at once commenced a steady retreat upon the camp, the Zulus being eight hundred yards when they opened fire, and rapidly lessening that distance.

On the left, Captain Shepstone soon realized the gravity of the situation, and found that the force which was first thought to be a detached body of small importance, was in reality the right horn of a Zulu army; and he rode back to report, and to ask for support or instructions. This was the turning-point of the day.

Even now, if the waggons, already inspanned, had been hastily *laagered*, merely drawn together, the oxen sent adrift, and the infantry

Plan No 1.

2 Troops Mount^d Natives under Col. Durnford. (left Camp abt 11 a.m. to reconnoitre.)

22nd. January 1879

donga (or stream)

Advance Column at 12.

Rocket Battery turned to left and went up.

small donga

High Hills

Road taken by General

large donga

2 Troops Mount^d Natives under Cap. Shepstone sent to reconnoitre about 10 a.m.

Picquet 1 Co 24th

N.N.C. N.M.P. R.A.

Isandhlwana Hill

Stony Kopje

Line of Retreat

Hills

Road to Rorke's Drift about 12 Miles

Scale ½ Inches = 1 Mile.

——— ROUGH SKETCH ———
TO ILLUSTRATE ISANDHLWANA
Positions from 10.30. A.M. to 11.30. A.M.
22nd. January 1879.

——— REFERENCE ———
24th Reg^t & R.A.
N.M. Police & Volunteers
Native Contingent
Zulus.
Guns.
Waggons.

collected inside with ammunition boxes, we should have been taught a sharp lesson, and should have had to deplore heavy loss, but not so terrible a disaster as that the tidings of which soon rang through South Africa and through the civilized world.

But about noon the die was cast, and two companies, under Captain Mostyn and Lieutenant Cavaye, were sent out to reinforce Shepstone's mounted natives on the left. Almost as soon, however, as the companies had come into action, it was found necessary for them to retire on the camp, because of the masses of the enemy which showed on their front and right front.

The position shortly after twelve o'clock was then as follows:—

To the front of the position, Durnford's mounted natives were retiring slowly on the camp before the Nkobamakosi and Umbonambi regiments, which must have numbered together nearly six thousand men, the Basutos taking advantage of every *donga* and defensible bit of ground to make a stand.

On the left, Shepstone's Basutos, supported by two companies 24th, were engaging a force of about eight thousand Zulus, composed of the Umcityu and Nokenke corps, and were retiring slowly before them on the camp; the fleet Zulus rapidly gaining on our men by rushing forward directly the fire slackened for a moment, which it necessarily did when the men turned about to retire.

By 12.30 Durnford's Basutos had reached, and were. holding firmly, the *donga* which was at the foot of the camp. There were near and in the *donga*, as well as the Basutos, the Natal volunteers and police, and two companies of the 24th, and the tremendous fire kept up by this force entirely checked the Zulu attack on our front.

It must be remembered that the Zulus were attacking from our left front, so that the Zulu centre was opposed to our left and left centre.

On the left of the troops fighting near and in the *donga*, and in rear nearer the camp, were two other companies of the 24th, fronting towards the left front of the camp—one in extended order, and one (Younghusband's) seemingly held in reserve. Near the first of these companies the guns were in action. The two companies on the left in support of Shepstone's Basutos had now reached to within about two hundred and fifty or three hundred yards of the camp, and had got into a tolerably close formation, but were very short of ammunition.

At this time the Zulu regiments in front, who were suffering so heavily from the fire of the troops in the *donga*, showed signs of wa-

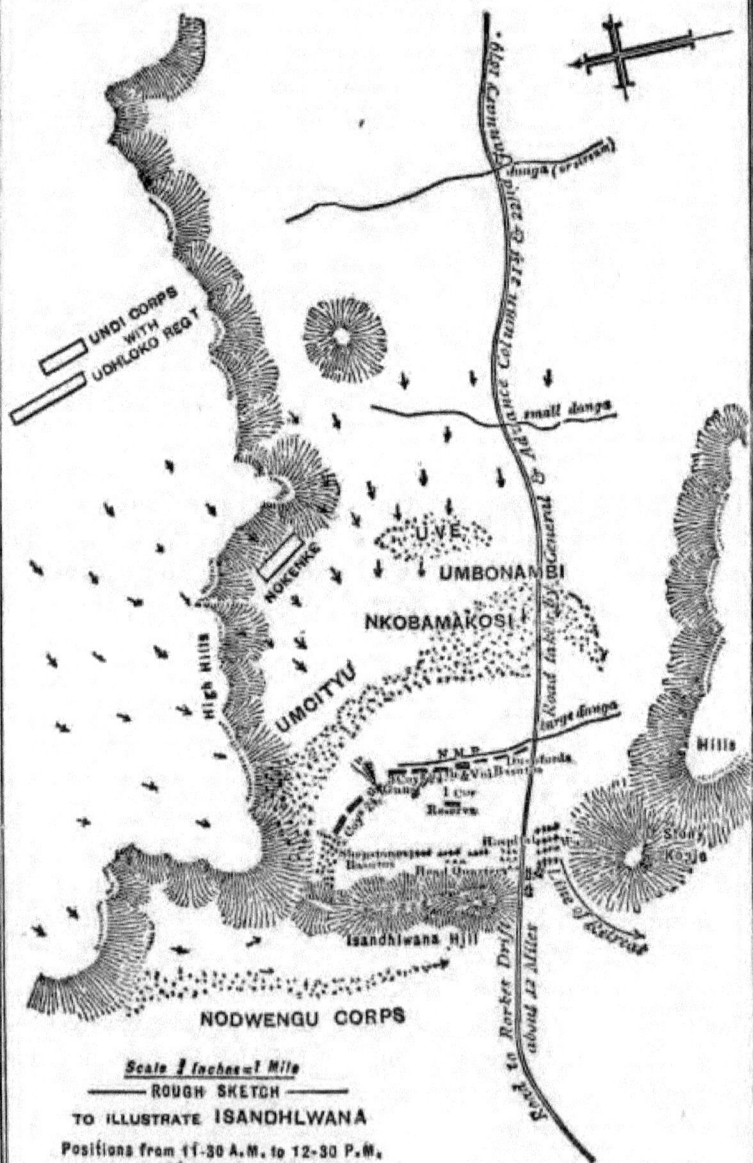

Plan Nº 2.

22nd January 1879.

Road taken by the General & Advance Column, 21st & 22nd January 1879.

donga (or stream)

small donga

UNDI CORPS
WITH
UDHLOKO REGT

U VE

UMBONAMBI

NKOBAMAKOSI

NOKENKE

High Hills

UMCITYU

large donga

Hills

N.N.B.

Rocket Battery & Vol Escorts

Isandhlwana Hill

Stony Koje

Line of Retreat

Road to Rorke's Drift about 12 Miles

NODWENGU CORPS

Scale ⅞ Inches = 1 Mile

ROUGH SKETCH

TO ILLUSTRATE ISANDHLWANA

Positions from 11-30 A.M. to 12-30 P.M.
22nd January 1879.

vering, and all seemed going well for the defenders of the camp. The men were as cheery as possible, those belonging to the two companies on the left retiring coolly, and quite convinced in their own minds that they had come back for more ammunition, and would turn the tables on the Umcityu when they had refilled their pouches and could fire more rapidly; for the ammunition of these two companies had been rapidly expended, owing to the hot fire they had been forced to sustain, to keep the Zulus from closing upon them while they were retreating on the camp.

But while the attention of the English soldiers had been taken up in fighting the centre and left of the Zulu army, the right horn of the Zulus was rapidly getting into a position from which to clutch its enemy in the rear.

Behind the range of hills on the left of the position the right horn, unseen and unthought-of, was warily and rapidly advancing. First, an officer, distinguished by his head ornament of leopard-skin, leading; then two or three warriors; then a cluster; then a continuous chain of men, thickening gradually as it stretched round toward the centre of the Zulu forces;—in this formation the Nodwengu corps, about four thousand strong, the men running and bounding in the air, encouraging one another with vehement gestures, silently made its way to the rear of the inaccessible hill, to take the doomed camp of the white men in reverse.

Just when the fire in the *donga* had begun slightly to slacken, and ammunition was being hurried out to all the companies, the leading warriors of the Nodwengu corps made their appearance round the inaccessible hill in the rear of the camp. This sudden appearance of the first few men who were leading the Zulu right must have sent a thrill of dismay through every white man who saw the enemy had got into their rear.

The moment the Zulu regiments in front caught sight of the point of their right horn, they steadied and recommenced their attack.

Their advance was most rapid and determined. Skirmishing in long lines ten or twelve deep, with men in closer formation a short distance behind, they closed on the camp regardless of their losses. When the guns fired, those Zulus towards whom the guns were laid would fall flat, let the shell pass over them, then spring up with a shout of "*Amoya!*" ("It is only wind"), and again rush onwards.

At this time the two companies of the 24th were on the edge of the left of the camp, still holding the Umcityu regiment in check; but

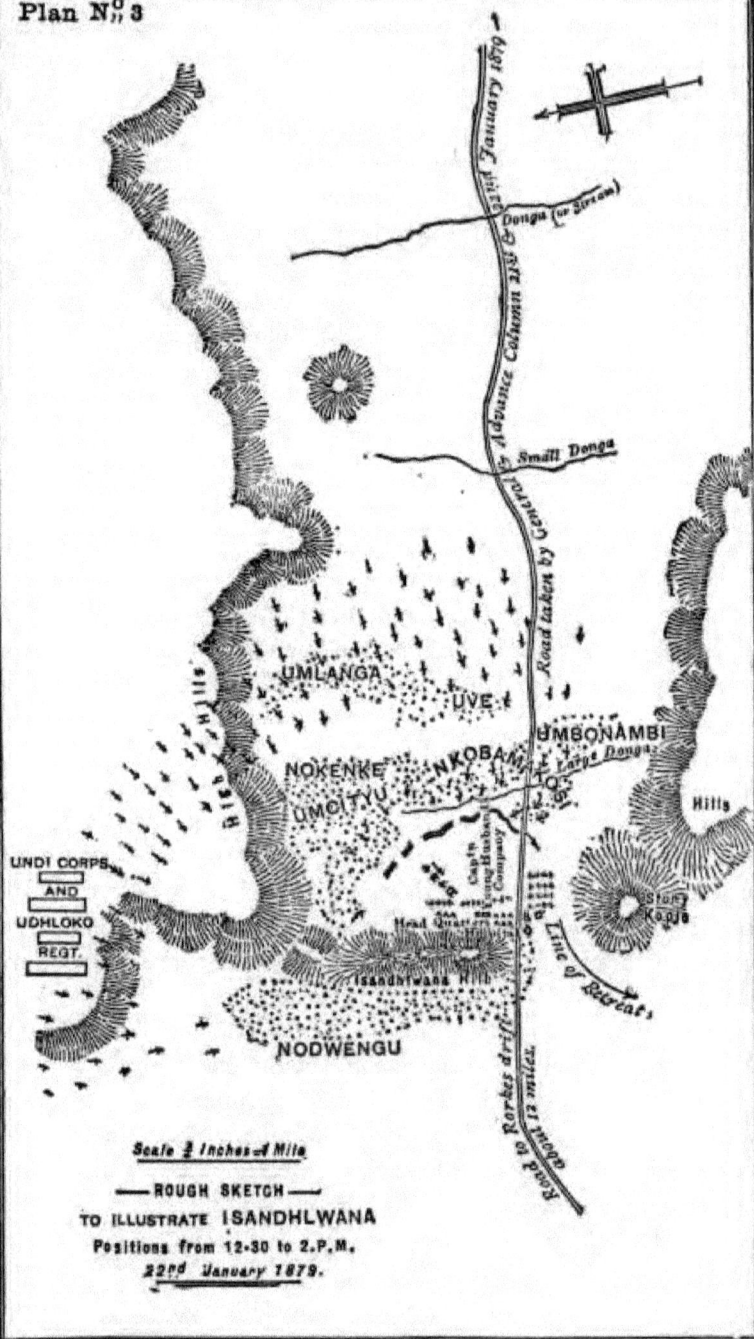

Plan No 3

Dongu (22nd January 1879)

Road taken by General & Advance Column 22nd January 1879

Dongu (or Spruit)

Small Donga

UMLANGA

UVE

UMBONAMBI

NOKENKE

NKOBAMA

Large Donga

UMCITYU

Hills

Capt. Young Husband Company

Stony Kopje

2nd Company

Head Quarters

UNDI CORPS
AND
UDHLOKO
REGT.

Isandhlwana

Line of Retreat

NODWENGU

Road to Rorke's drift about 12 miles

Scale ¾ Inches = 1 Mile

— ROUGH SKETCH —

TO ILLUSTRATE ISANDHLWANA

Positions from 12·30 to 2.P.M.

22nd January 1879.

on the right the Umbonambi regiment, having separated itself from the Nkobamakosi and Uve, who were directly in front of the *donga*, made a determined rush into the camp on the right, and, keeping to their own right, took the troops who had been in the *donga*, and who were endeavouring to retire for ammunition to the waggons, in flank. At the same time the Umcityu charged the two companies on the left, and the Nodwengu poured in from the rear. The ranks of our men were thrown into more disorder by the men of the Native Contingent rushing away to endeavour to escape from their dreaded enemy, and the whole camp became one thick mass of Zulus surging in overwhelming numbers round the white men, fighting by companies, groups, or even singly.

The mounted Basutos, having managed to get their docile and hardy ponies out of the *donga*, fired two or three rounds at a point where the Zulus seemed weakest, and then charged, and many of them managed to escape.

The 24th, police, and volunteers were all endeavouring to close together, and to fight their way to the waggons for ammunition.

Younghusband's company, which has already been spoken of as having been held somewhat in reserve, was seemingly in square, and, with pouches tolerably full, was retiring steadily higher up the hill, drawing to it any stragglers who could reach it, and having the bandsmen of the regiment and the colours of the 2-24th in its centre.

The guns had been limbered up shortly before the charge of the Zulus, and had endeavoured to make their way from the left to the right of the camp; then, finding the road to Rorke's Drift barred, tried to discover a way of escape down the rocky valley leading to the Buffalo. But it was too late. As the guns charged through the Zulus, the gunners were *assegai*ed on the limbers and the drivers on the horses. One gun was upset, Major Smith, who was killed near the bank of the Buffalo half an hour afterwards, being wounded in a gallant but ineffectual attempt to spike it; the horses of the other, maddened with pain and terror, galloped away towards a deep ravine about half a mile from the camp, and were found there afterwards, hanging stiff and stark in their harness over the precipice.

Of the desperate hand-to-hand combat now fought out to the last by the old and tried soldiers of the 24th and the brave little band of colonial troops, against overwhelming numbers, we shall never know the exact details. We can only form an idea of what occurred from those who caught a hurried glimpse of the scene while making their escape, and from the accounts of the Zulus themselves, weighing both by the sad evidence afforded by the position of our dead.

When the Umcityu and Nokenke regiments charged the two companies commanded by Mostyn and Cavaye, as they had just reached the camp the ranks turned back to back, and they fought sternly out to the end with the bayonet, without attempting to retire further.

"The red soldiers who had been out on the left," said an officer of the Umcityu, "they killed many of us with their bayonets. When they found we were upon them, they turned back to back. They all fought till they died. They were hard to kill; not one tried to escape."

One company, it is not clear which, seemed to have determined to cut its road through to Rorke's Drift, and by dint of desperate efforts and losing many men on its way, got on to and past the neck; but, weakened by its losses, it could get no further, and here a heap of gallant dead marked where its last stand was made.

While this company was fighting its way to the neck, Younghusband's taking up a position under Isandhlwana Hill, and Mostyn and Cavaye's being overwhelmed by the Umcityu, the two remaining companies under Wardell were, with the Natal police and volunteers, struggling together against the masses of the enemy, almost in the centre of the camp.

The Zulus, with keen and ready appreciation of gallantry, tell many tales of the way our men struggled on, fighting to the last, and how hard they struck before they could be subdued.

One tall man, a corporal of the 24th, killed four Zulus with his bayonet, but his weapon stuck for an instant in the throat of his last opponent, and the Zulus rushed in on him.

The only sailor in the camp, one of the men of Her Majesty's ship *Active*, was seen, his back against a waggon wheel, keeping the Zulus at bay with his cutlass; but a Zulu crept behind him, and stabbed him through the spokes.

One of the Natal volunteers, who had been sick in hospital, was found with his back against a stone near the hospital tent, nearly a hundred fired cartridges round him, his revolver empty, and his bowie-knife clutched in his hand.

Another quarter of an hour, at about half-past one, and the scene has again changed. Except on the slopes close below the inaccessible hill, every white man is down among heaps of the enemy. The Zulus who have not been to pillage have their attention turned to one point.

Below the inaccessible hill, as high up on its slopes as possible, is collected the remnant of the 24th. The company already mentioned as fighting in company square, having drawn to it a few stragglers and one or two officers who until now have escaped the *assegai*, has chosen the ground on which it means to die. It must have been quite clear to them that there was for them no chance of escape. There was only one point from which help could come, and the country could be seen for miles in that direction. Ammunition must have been then running low, and it was impossible for a fresh supply to be obtained, while the Zulu regiments were in swarms and in thousands round the hill. The Zulus (for no white man saw the end) tell the story—how firm the red soldiers stood; they describe the officers calling out and encouraging their men; they tell how often they charged the little square, till they became, after their heavy losses through the day, somewhat reluctant to attack it; they tell how the red soldiers even taunted them by gestures to come on; and then how at last, the white man's ammunition running short, they flung showers of *assegais*, standing just out of reach of the bayonet, and then rushed in and finished the one-sided fight

"Ah, those red soldiers at Isandhlwana!" many Zulus have said; "how few they were, and how they fought! They fell like stones, each man in his place."

But all the Zulu army was not occupied in breaking the 24th square, or in pillaging. The rugged valley leading to Rorke's Drift was full of them and of fugitives from the camp, mostly natives, mixed up with camp-followers, non-combatants, and mounted men. Down this little valley, which had for years probably never witnessed anything more exciting than a hawk pinioning a song-bird, or a Zulu lad searching for a lost ox, many started against the Zulus in a hard race for life.

On the English side there were but few winners.

Shortly after noon, when the Zulu right horn showed in the rear of the hill, an effort was made to save the Queen's colour of the 1-24th. Their regimental colour was not on the field, but was at Helpmaaker camp with two companies of the regiment. The colour had been probably in charge of the company which had acted during the morning as a reserve; and now when the case seemed a desperate one and the camp all but taken, the colour was handed over to Melvill, the adjutant of the battalion, and he started, accompanied by Colonel Glyn's orderly officer, Nevill Coghill, who had been left in camp that day owing to a sprained knee. They managed to cut their way out of camp, and fell into the stream of fugitives and of Zulus in the valley. Here they overtook Private Williams, Colonel Glyn's groom, on a spare horse of his master's.

In consequence of the bad ground, steep and rocky and strewn with boulders, it was impossible to get any speed out of the horses, and the Zulus kept up with the fugitives without much difficulty, and a running fight was carried on the whole way to the river.

Before long Coghill's horse was wounded and his saddle slipped. Private Williams dismounted, and helped him to resaddle and remount his horse, this delay bringing the Zulus very near.

The three reached the riverside close together, Melvill being a little in advance.

Private Williams had to jump his horse where the bank was high and the water deep, and went under water with his horse, being carried some way down stream; and when, after a long struggle, he reached the Natal bank, he saw neither Melvill nor Coghill.

Melvill's horse was shot in the stream, and probably, in endeavouring to extricate himself from the dying animal, the colour got out of his grasp.

Coghill had reached the Natal bank in safety, but on seeing Melvill clinging to a rock in the river, trying to recover the colour, he rode back into the river to his assistance. Here *his* horse was shot.

Not until the Zulus were close upon them did they give up the endeavour to regain the colour.

But it was too late.

They both reached the Natal bank, and struggled together some three hundred yards up the rocky *kloof* leading from the river, and then found their pursuers gaining on them, and themselves so exhausted by their desperate ride and struggles in the water, that they could go no further.

There are, not many hundred yards from the riverside, two boulders within six feet of each other, near the rocky path. At these boulders they made their last stand and fought until overwhelmed. Here we found them lying side by side, and buried them on the spot where they fought and fell so gallantly.

There is no need of anything to remind Englishmen of this story. While we remember the Zulu war it will not be forgotten; but that the place where Melville and Coghill fell should be securely marked, a stone cross has erected, and stands watching the lonely spot.

These words are upon it:—

"For Queen and Country."

———

in memory of
Lieutenant and Adjutant Teignmouth Melvill
and Lieutenant Nevill J. S. Coghill,
1st Battalion, 24th Regiment,
Who died on this spot the 22nd January, 1879,
To save the Queen's Colour of their Regiment.
"Jesu, mercy."

They did not die in vain; ten days after they fell, the colour was found in the rocky bed of the Buffalo.

CHAPTER 9

Rorke's Drift

To return to the force bivouacking on Isandhlwana Neck. We were lying in a hollow square, the native battalions being posted on the kopjes on our right and left.

The men were wearied out, and it was a great relief for them to lie down and know that, as the Zulus never attacked until after midnight, they would probably get some rest before they had to cut their way to Rorke's Drift.

For it seemed to us, after hearing the accounts of the overwhelming force of the Zulu *impi* and its complete success, that the victorious Zulus were only waiting their usual time for attack (shortly before dawn) to endeavour to complete the destruction of No. 2 Column.

The night wore on. Some of the officers took snatches of sleep, some talked in low voices; the men lay tired out by their long day's marching, during which they must have covered over thirty-two or thirty-three miles.

The first part of the night was very black and dark, but about one a.m. the sky cleared and the stars shone out, and I received orders to serve out the rations of biscuit and tinned meat we luckily had with us.

It was disagreeable work moving about inside the square; in the dark it was difficult to walk without stumbling over the dead and the debris of all kinds with which the ground was strewn.

After the regulars and volunteers had drawn their rations, the officers and non-commissioned officers of the Natal Contingent came for theirs. One officer—I could not see his face and have no notion who he was—asked leave to draw for six or seven of his comrades, and as he had forgotten to bring a haversack, and could not carry six or seven rations of loose biscuit and tinned meat in his hands, I told him he had better hold out his hat for the biscuit. "Sir," said he stiffly, "I must object to your suggestion. I should prefer to go without my rations than carry them in my hat." As it then seemed highly probable that before long there would not be many of us with either a head to put a hat on or a mouth to put a biscuit into, and as there was not any time to waste, I sent this gentleman away in a hurry to fetch someone else to draw rations; and in case he reads these lines, I beg to tender him my apologies if my words seemed to him more curt than is allowable on ordinary occasions.

Shortly after rations had been issued—not very long before dawn, but while it was still quite dark—a yell was heard from below the kopje on our right, where was posted a battalion of the Native Contingent; then a rush of naked feet and the rattle of *assegais* and shields, and the clatter of accoutrements and rifles of the men in the ranks as they rose from the ground, and then a confused volley.

It seemed as if the attack we had been expecting had come at last The men in square were quite steady—the 24th not firing a shot, but merely rising to the knee; the artillery standing to their horses. After a few anxious minutes it was found to be a false alarm, caused by the native battalion on the right running in upon the square, fancying the Zulus were advancing.

When the first streak of dawn gave enough light to enable the track to be seen, the column, or rather the remains of it, resumed its march. It was bitter leaving the bodies of our comrades still unburied, but the living had to be thought of first. Even if we had had ammunition and ration waggons with us, the fires we could see on the Natal side of the Buffalo showed plainly that the Zulus were in Natal, and we were bound to hurry back to assist in protecting the colony.

Dawn in South Africa breaks quickly, and before the rear-guard, with which my duties lay, left the ridge, there was light enough to show the state of the camp and what had been concealed by the darkness. It was a sight not easily forgotten.

During the first two hours of our march our path lay through broken and hilly ground, and we expected, before we reached the open country, that an attack would be made upon us.

None, however, occurred, and we arrived at the other side of the little Bashee Spruit (at which the men were glad to drink and refill their water-bottles) without interference.

Till then we had hardly time to realize what had happened; it had seemed so very unlikely that the Zulus would forego the advantages offered by attacking a tired force bivouacking in an enclosed country, after they had been so completely victorious in their first onset, that we had been speculating on the future more than thinking on the past

But now, when we got into the open ground and found our way open to Rorke's Drift, we had time to think of those we had left behind on that fatal ridge, and a host of familiar faces rose to our recollection with a tightening of the heart as we rode along.

Soon we saw that the post at Rorke's Drift was on fire, and feared the worst, and made sure that at any rate the ponts had been wrecked.

We advanced on the river, and our scouts, to the surprise of all, reported the ponts standing. The cavalry crossed below them at the shallows, as it had done twelve days before, and the first files advanced up to where the mission station had stood, at the best gallop their weary and hungry horses could muster after having been under the saddle nearly thirty hours.

We expected to find a repetition on a smaller scale of Isandhlwana camp, but as we came in sight of the commissariat stores, a cheer sounded from the top of a wall of *mealie* sacks, from a man on the lookout, and was taken up by the remainder of the little garrison, and to our delight we found that there was no more bad news to be expected, at any rate at present.

To relate what had occurred here we must retrace our steps.

About 2.30 that afternoon, when the sack of Isandhlwana was complete, when the Zulu regiments who had been engaged were scattered all over the camp—some helping themselves to booty and ammunition; some stabbing each dead man, so that the corpse should not swell (the Zulu superstition is that if this is not done, as the body swells and corrupts, the right hand and arm of its slayer also swells and corrupts); some carrying away those wounded Zulus who could be moved, and shooting those who could not; some throwing their dead into holes, ravines, and *dongas*;—about this time the Undi corps, the crack corps of the Zulu army (which, with the exception of the Nkobamakosi regiment, which had already been heavily engaged, had been held in reserve), arrived, fresh and eager for fighting, in the camp.

Finding there was nothing for them to do here, and being ignorant that the whole of the column was not destroyed, this corps continued its march in the direction of the Buffalo. After crossing, the corps split up into regiments. The crack regiment, the royal Tulwana, in whose ranks Cetywayo had fought in his younger days, and to which he still nominally belonged, advanced to attack Rorke's Drift, accompanied by portions of three other regiments, making up a force of between three and four thousand men. The other portions of the Undi corps dispersed in search of plunder and cattle.

At Rorke's Drift, as has been before mentioned, there was stationed, to guard the ponts, stores, and hospital, the B company of the second battalion 24th, under Lieutenant Bromhead. The ponts were in charge of Lieutenant Chard, R.E.

News of the disaster at Isandhlwana reached these officers about three p.m., and they began at once hurriedly strengthening their position.

A worse position could hardly be imagined. Two small thatched buildings, about thirty-nine yards apart, with thin walls, commanded by rising ground on the south and west, completely overlooked on the south by a high hill. On the north side an orchard and garden gave good cover to an enemy up to within a few yards of the houses.

The force which was about to defend this position against three or four thousand Zulus consisted of one hundred and four officers and men, and thirty-five sick.

The commander of the Undi corps, Dabulamanzi, a brother of the king—a fierce, ambitious, and able man—did not give this little force much time to prepare for their reception.

All hands worked hard for about two hours at loopholing and barricading the buildings, and joining the two houses by parapets formed out of a few waggons, sacks of *mealies*, and biscuit boxes. There was barely time to complete these hurried preparations for defence, when the enemy made his appearance round the hill to the south, and the advance-guard charged down the slope towards the parapet, the main body occupying the cliffs overlooking the position. The Zulus got within fifty yards of the wall, but were checked by the heavy fire which met them, and turned off to their right and left—some taking up good positions on the hill for firing into the *laager*; others, taking advantage of the cover afforded by the garden and orchard, making a determined rush at the parapet.

For the next two hours, fierce assaults on that side of the *laager* where cover was to be found were incessant, and were repelled by the defenders as much by the bayonet as by musketry.

While the assaults had been going on, the enemy had been attempting to force the hospital, and the sick had to be moved.

In performing this difficult duty. Privates Williams, Hook, Rich-

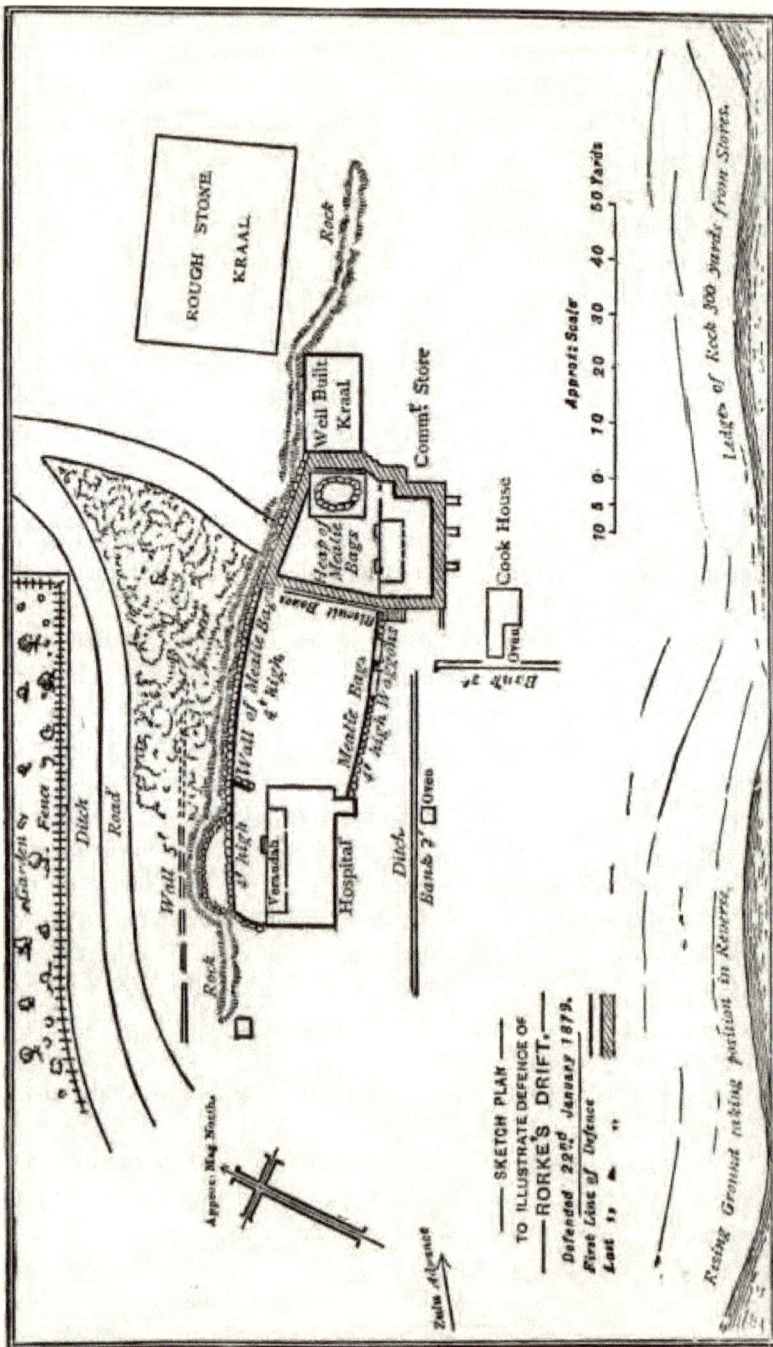

ROUGH STONE KRAAL.

Well Built Kraal

Comm: Store

Cook House

Heap of Mealie Bags

Mealie Bags 4' high Wagonet:

Hospital

Verandah

5' high

Wall of Mealie Bags 4' high

Biscuit Boxes

Oven

Bank 2'

Ditch

Bank 2'

Oven

Garden

Fence 2'

Ditch

Road

Wall 5'

Rock

Rock

Rock

Appro: Mag North

Zulu Assegais

Ledges of Rock 300 yards from Stores.

Resting Ground taking position in Reserve.

SKETCH PLAN
TO ILLUSTRATE DEFENCE OF
RORKE'S DRIFT,
Defended 22nd January 1879.

First Line of Defence
Last "   "

Appro: Scale

10 5 0   10   20   30   40   50 Yards

ard and William Jones behaved with the utmost coolness and bravery, fighting desperately with the enemy from room to room, taking it in turn to hold the doors while the others carried or assisted out the sick. One poor fellow, who was delirious, was twice carried into a place of safety, but ran back and was *assegai*ed by the enemy.

The enemy set fire to the hospital when it was abandoned, which proved of great assistance in directing the fire of the garrison.

Up to midnight the enemy did not slacken in their attempts to carry the position, the officer in command shouting his orders to his men from under the rocky hill overlooking it.

The bravery and recklessness of death of the Zulus was beyond belief. Men would rush up to the parapet, leap up and clutch the muzzle of a rifle, and endeavour to pull themselves up by it; others would try to pull down the *mealie* sacks. Again and again assaults were made on the *laager* from different points, and only repulsed after hard hand-to-hand fighting; the men in some cases actually wresting the *assegais* from the Zulus, and killing them with their own weapons.

After much desperate fighting, the little garrison, being completely surrounded, had to retire to an inner circle of *mealie* sacks, which had been formed as a sort of citadel, being obliged to abandon their first line of parapet. Here, throughout the night, they maintained their position, and their fire being guided by the flames of bundles of thatch, and from the blazing hospital, were able to inflict much loss on the enemy.

About four o'clock the Zulu fire ceased, and they began carrying off their dead and wounded; and when It was light enough to see, the enemy was found to be slowly retiring over the hill whence they had come.

When day broke, the scene must have been a startling one. The blackened and roofless hospital still burning, and flames still darting from the heaps of thatch. Hundreds of Zulus lying round the buildings and parapets in every conceivable attitude and posture. In some places they had fallen in heaps one over the other—some with the most ghastly wounds, from having been so close to the muzzle of the rifle which killed them; others having been consumed by fire, from having fallen into the flames of the hospital, as they were killed or wounded. The 24th men, all blackened, torn, and weary, many wounded and bleeding, some dead or dying.

The enemy having retired, patrols were sent out from the garrison to collect the arms of the Zulus and to examine the ground. It was found that the wounded Zulus, expecting to be killed, were as dangerous to go near as wild animals in a trap, and some of our men narrowly escaped being injured by wounded Zulus clutching at them suddenly as they passed, endeavouring to seize their rifles and *assegai* them.

At this time an artilleryman was brought into the *laager*, who had had a wonderful escape. He had been in the hospital when the sick were ordered to quit the building, and being weak and ill he got confused, and ran out in the darkness in the wrong direction, and found himself outside the *laager* amongst the Zulus, instead of inside the *laager* amongst his friends. He threw himself on the ground, behind a bush, concealing himself with grass and branches as well as he could. He was equally exposed to the Zulu *assegais* and the English bullets. His greatest anxiety was to cover the red stripe of his overalls, which seemed to him to show very clearly through the darkness. He was very nearly discovered several times—once from the complaints and remonstrances of a stray pig, who had been struck down close to him by a chance bullet, and whose acclamations attracted attention.

When it was certain that the enemy had really retired, the garrison began to strengthen their shattered defences. About seven o'clock, while thus employed, another body of Zulus appeared on the hills, advancing as if to the attack. Luckily the worst had passed. The remains of No. 3 Column appeared now within a short distance of the river, and on this the Zulus changed direction and retired, making the best of their way back into Zulu Land.

The loss sustained by the garrison of Rorke's Drift was seventeen killed and ten wounded—twenty-seven casualties out of one hundred and thirty-nine men.

There were over three hundred dead Zulus lying close round the parapets and buildings. Their actual loss we shall never know; but it must have far exceeded five hundred, as very many bodies were carried away and thrown into *dongas* by the Zulus.

Such, then, were the memorable actions of Isandhlwana and Rorke's Drift.

At Isandhlwana our own loss in killed was unfortunately too easily calculated; the survivors could be almost counted on the fingers. Twenty- seven officers of the regular army, twenty-two officers of the colonial forces, and seven hundred and seventy-five non-commissioned officers and men were left on that fatal field. Our loss in material was very heavy. One stand of colours, two guns, nearly seven hundred stand of arms, between ninety and one hundred waggons, containing large quantities of ammunition, fell into the enemy's hands.

The Zulu losses at Isandhlwana are extremely difficult to ascertain, but they were acknowledged by the Zulus to have been very heavy.

The Umcityu corps, which attacked the two companies of the 24th, under Captain Mostyn and Lieutenant Cavaye, on the extreme left of our position, suffered terribly. These companies fought, it appears, in two ranks, back to back, and even after their ammunition was suspended, inflicted with the bayonet severe loss on the Umcityu, whose loss is estimated at eight hundred.

One of the regiments of the Undi corps, the Nkobamakosi, which was opposed to the troops holding the *donga*, was mowed down by the fire which met it as it endeavoured to advance, and was entirely checked until the flank of the *donga* was turned by the charge of the Umbonambi.

Both these regiments were considered to have lost about six hundred apiece, and there were other regiments which were considered to have lost nearly as heavily.

Probably the Zulu loss (always including the wounded who died in their *kraals*) was between two thousand six hundred and three thousand.

The Zulu army began to disperse directly after Isandhlwana, many returning straight from the field of battle with their booty to their *kraals*. This was contrary to orders, but the severe fighting and the amount of booty which had fallen into their hands had entirely disorganized the Zulu regiments.

The Undi—the royal corps—however, preserved its discipline, and after sullenly and unwillingly retreating from Rorke's Drift, marched straight to Ulundi.

The king, according to custom, received them in the grand *kraal*.

He had only as yet received the news that the white man's camp had been taken, and that "Somtseu's" column had been eaten up. He had not heard of the repulse at Rorke's Drift, nor was he prepared for the terrible gaps made in his regiments. As the men began to file into the enclosure, he saw there had been very different fighting to that he had known in the Amaswazi and Amatonga country.

The Tulwana was the last regiment, and it filed in and saluted. "Why don't the rest come in?" cried the king, impatiently. But the rest of the brave Tulwana could not hear him, for they were lying outside the *mealie* bags and biscuit boxes at Rorke's Drift.

CHAPTER 10

Requiem

The Zulu force which was despatched by the king against No. 1,
or General Pearson's column, reached the position it was to occupy to
bar the advance of the white men on the evening of the 16th of January. The position chosen by the Zulus showed sound judgment The
Zulus were posted in some reeds and thick bush, where the track began to rise up out of the valley of the Amatikulu, and were distributed
in such a formation that they could attack the right flank and envelop
the head of the column in a front attack at the same time.

The regiments composing this force consisted of the Umxapo, "the
sprinklers;" the Ngulusi, "the pigs;" and the Nsugamgeni regiment,
and a few hundred Zulus from the *kraals* close by. The total strength of
the force was about four thousand five hundred men.

The force at General Pearson's disposal consisted of 200 blue-jackets and marines, with a Gatling gun and two 7-pounders R.A.; 300
volunteer cavalry and mounted infantry, under Major Barrow; about
1500 infantry (the second battalion of the Buffs and six companies of
the 99th), and two battalions of natives, numbering about 2000 men.
There was also a company of Royal Engineers with this column.

The troops comprising No. 1 Column were all safely on the Zulu
bank of the Tugela by Monday, the 13th of January, but many of the
waggons belonging to the column were still on the Natal bank, and
there was considerable difficulty experienced in getting them across
speedily.

The Tugela was here about three hundred yards wide, and the
weather boisterous, and the working of the ponts under these conditions proved slow and tedious.

It was not until the 18th of January that the column was able to
march away from the riverbank and reach the Inioni River, a little

stream about ten miles from the Tugela,

Two days were occupied in crossing the Amatikulu River, in the neighbourhood of which the bush is thick and the road heavy. By dint of hard work the column encamped on the north bank of the river on the evening of the 21st of January.

At daybreak on the 22nd, the troops commenced moving up out of the valley of the Amatikulu.

After three hours' marching a halt was ordered for the men to get their breakfasts, and the waggons at the head of column commenced to form up into *laager*. Just at this time the advanced scouts reported the enemy in front, and almost at once the Zulu attack on the front and right flank commenced.

The front attack developed quickly, the Zulus skirmishing with great rapidity and advancing to within one hundred and fifty yards of the position where the head of the column had commenced *laagering*. Two 7-pounders R.A. and two rocket tubes of the Naval Brigade were at once brought into action, and two companies of the Naval Brigade and two companies of the Buffs at once opened a heavy fire to meet the attack on the front and right front. The enemy were checked, but, from the road being much commanded, were enabled to keep up an effective fire from various knolls and *kopjes*. It was found necessary to dislodge them, and the Buffs and blue-jackets gallantly charged the position the enemy had taken up, driving them back with loss.

In the meantime two more companies of the Buffs, with the marines and the Gatling, were hotly engaged in resisting the flank attack on the Zulus, which they did with great success.

The Zulus had expected that the column would have been thrown into confusion by their sudden attack, and that the waggons would halt and get into disorder. The rear waggons, however, moved steadily on, each waggon *laagering* as soon as it reached the front, and the column of route got shorter and shorter, successive detachments of infantry, which had been employed on waggon escort, being set free to assist in driving back the enemy.

By eleven o'clock the enemy was in full retreat on all sides, leaving no wounded, but three hundred dead on the field. Our loss consisted of twelve men killed and eighteen wounded. No officers were wounded, but General Pearson and Colonel Parnell, of the Buffs, both had their horses shot under them.

It will be seen that the Zulus were defeated by a part only of No. 1 Column, and that their style of fighting was very different from the dash and determination of the crack Zulu regiments—the Undi corps or the brave Umcityu, for instance.

The force at the battle of Inyesane, as this action was called, was, in fact, composed of regiments raised in the coast districts, and the Zulu clans or tribes inhabiting the coast line cannot vie with those who live in the vicinity of the king's *kraal* for fighting qualities, nor have they that prestige and *esprit de corps* which the regiments engaged at Isandhlwana possessed, and which, combined with their discipline, made them so irresistible to the British in the weak and scattered formation in which our soldiers endeavoured to meet them.

After the action No. 1 Column continued its march, and early on the 23rd reached Ekowe mission station. It was here that the news of the Isandhlwana disaster reached General Pearson, and, after a consultation "with his staff and commanding officers, he decided to stand his ground and await in this position the arrival of the reinforcements from England, which would enable the advance on Ulundi to be recommenced. General Pearson had over two months' provisions with him, and this supply, with what could be obtained, it was hoped, by raiding parties, would enable them to hold out until reinforced. The two native battalions and the mounted men under Major Barrow were sent back to Natal, and a strong entrenched position was at once commenced.

While the events already described had been taking place, in which General Pearson's, Colonel Durnford's (No. 2), and Colonel Glyn's columns had been concerned, No. 4, General Evelyn Wood's column, had been reconnoitring across the Blood River in the direction of the head waters of the White Umvolosi.

General Wood's column consisted of Tremlett's battery of artillery, of the 13th and 90th Light Infantry, numbering together about fifteen hundred bayonets, and about two hundred mounted men under Colonel Redvers Buller. There was also a small battalion of native infantry, numbering between three or four hundred men.

Last, but not least, there was a small corps of Dutch *burghers*, numbering forty or fifty men, under Mr. Piet Uys.

The attitude of most of the Transvaal Boers on the Zulu border towards the English Government, was in most cases one of sullen neutrality. As regards the Zulu question, "they would not," they said, "come forward to help the English. Let them fight the Zulus themselves. They had taken the Transvaal; let them defend it."

This was the answer to any who endeavoured to obtain mounted *burghers* for service against the Zulus.

Such was not the view of Piet Uys and of those who stood by him. "Whether we approve or not of the annexation of the Transvaal is beside the matter now," said he and those who thought with him. "The English are fighting our national enemy; it is a question of white against black, of Christian against heathen. Are we to stand aloof as if we had no interest in the matter?"

Piet Uys brought, then, to General Wood's camp a force small in numbers, but each man possessed of great experience in Zulu tactics and strategy.

Piet Uys himself came of fighting blood. His father, another Piet Uys, with a son, a boy of twelve, by his side, fell fighting hand to hand against the warriors of Dingaan. The boy, fighting bravely, died by his father's side.

General Wood had various skirmishes with the enemy, during which the Zulus suffered considerable loss; but the force of four thousand men who were sent to attack No. 4 Column, never having been allowed a chance of attacking the column at a disadvantage, owing to the good scouting of the mounted men under Colonel Buller, after watching and lying in wait for the column for some time, dispersed a few days after Isandhlwana..

After the 22nd of January, General Wood retired his column to a. strong position at Kambula Hill, whence he could cover both Newcastle and Utrecht, giving confidence to both the Natal and Transvaal borders.

His column was, however, kept by no means on the passive defensive, and the perpetual raids and harassing expeditions carried out by his. orders by Colonel Buller with his mounted men, and with the, Dutch, *burghers* under Mr. Piet Uys, made him the terror of the robber chiefs in the neighbourhood, and formed the one satisfactory subject to talk or think about during the weary weeks which passed after Isandhlwana, until the arrival of the reinforcements.

We left No. 3 Column on the morning of the 23rd of January, about half-past eight, recrossing the Buffalo River. The crossing this time did not take long. Harness's four guns and waggons, and one mule waggon, which had carried the biscuit, comprised our wheeled vehicles.

By half-past nine, the remains of No. 3 Column had marched up to Rorke's Drift, and were getting their breakfasts round the shattered buildings and temporary parapet, which for twelve hours had sustained so desperate an attack. This over, all hands set to work in setting things to rights; while the headquarters staff, the mounted men, and Harness's four guns continued their march to Helpmakaar.

One of the most necessary duties to be undertaken was the burial of the dead and the cleansing of the ground. This had to be taken in hand without a moment's delay, as decomposition comes on quickly under the hot African sun. The superintendence of this work happened to be my duty.

The Native Contingent battalions were still with the column, though many had already deserted to their homes. There were, however, a sufficient number of them to supply a strong working party, which was at once set digging a pit about four hundred yards from the stores. The natives have a great repugnance to touching a dead body, so the soldiers had to do this part of the work. If we had had a few carts, or even horses, our labours would have been much lightened, but the dead Zulus had either to be hauled by "*reims*" (ropes of hide) over the ground, or carried in rough stretchers.

It was disagreeable work handling the dead, naked, bodies, many with awful looking wounds.

The men worked hard and cheerfully, and we soon got the immediate neighbourhood of the entrenchment clear of dead bodies.

"Come on, you black devil," I heard a man mutter to a dead Zulu he was hauling over the grass, as the body caught against a stone; "I'm blamed if you don't give more trouble dead nor alive."

"It's your turn now, comrade, now we've cleared the rubbish out of your way," said another 24th man to a dead soldier, who was found with two or three Zulus stretched almost upon him. "I'm main sorry to put you away, mate," continued he, laying the end of a torn sack gently over the dead man's face, "but you died well and had a soldier's end."

Homely words, but what soldier could wish a better requiem? The dead of the little garrison were buried where the colonist who gave his name to the drift lies, and the burial service was read over them by the chaplain.

Though most of the dead Zulus were buried by the 24th, it was very hard to get at the dead bodies of the men who had crept away into the long grass, mortally wounded, to die, and for days and days afterwards bodies of men would be found, which had defied previous search.

Only two or three wounded men were found, and these were taken care of and treated by the surgeons of the force. There were never probably many; but though strict orders were given on the subject, it was impossible to prevent the Natal natives, who were slipping away to their homes, killing, according to their custom, any wounded they came across on their way.

There seemed at one time in South Africa a persistent endeavour of some persons to spread rumours pointing to the cruel and brutal treatment by our soldiers of any Zulus who fell into our hands. What end such rumours had, it is hard to understand.

The fact is, that no more difficult task was ever cheerfully imposed on themselves by British officers than that in the Zulu war—to preserve the high reputation of the British army of forbearance to an enemy who asks or who will receive quarter.

When it is remembered that even to count the dead after an action with the Zulus was a service of considerable danger, on account of the wounded Zulus attacking unawares those engaged in this duty, and that in some cases it was on this account actually forbidden, some idea will be formed of the difficulty in extending to the brave but savage enemy precisely the same rules that are observed in civilized warfare.

Wars against a savage and uncivilized enemy must always be more or less brutalizing, but it may safely be said that as no soldiers in Europe but ours can be made to remain in civil riots under abuse and blows without retaliating, so no soldiers but ours could have come so clean-handed out of a conflict such as has just been concluded in South Africa.

Particular efforts were at one time made to blacken the character of the remainder of No. 3 Column which had returned to Rorke's Drift, with accusations of having put an end to the wounded Zulus who had been left on the ground when the Zulus retired, after their attempt to carry the *laager*.

In the first place, the Zulus retired with considerable deliberation, and carried off most of their wounded with them. If any wounded were to be killed, our men would not have had a chance of acting up to the character of brutality it has been desired to foist on to them; for the Natal Native Contingent, dispersing to their homes after Isandhlwana, passed at right angles to the line of retreat of the Tulwana regiment, and right over the ground where the action had taken place, and if any wounded men were then alive they would have been put an end to, according to native custom.

I myself saw three wounded Zulus at Rorke's Drift. Two of them were found on the morning of the 23rd, and were brought in by some men of the 24th and treated by one of the surgeons of the column; the third was found half-starving in a *kraal* some days afterwards, having crept there disabled by a leg wound.

If the Zulus were questioned on the point they would express their astonishment at the clemency of the British.

The Zulus showed the utmost confidence in our good faith, and, under a white flag, would come fearlessly into a camp which they proposed attacking in a few hours.

It may not be known that in the old colony war, if the Kafirs were getting the worst of it, it was not uncommon for the women of the tribe to run forward to cover the retreat of the men, secure that the fire of the *"ama johnnies"* would cease. So common had this become, that if it was suspected there were women in bush that had to be cleared, the commander would sometimes shout to them to come out before he commenced firing, and the women would come out with their bundles in the most unconcerned way—even interchange rough jokes with our men as they passed through the line of skirmishers to the rear.

Such conduct tallies but ill with accounts of the cruelty of the British soldier, and if we allowed comparisons to influence us we might compare such, without concern for our own reputation, with the behaviour of other continental soldiery—with that of the Russians in Central Asia, or of the French in Algiers.

For the first few days the men were rather miserable. We had lost everything at Isandhlwana; blankets and great-coats, as well as everything else, had been swept off by the Zulus. We had some wet nights, which, as the men had to lie down on the ground with no shelter, and with nothing more on than they wore in the day, was trying enough.

However, tarpaulin shelter and blankets were obtained as soon as possible from Helpmakaar, a *depôt* of stores on the line of communications, about twelve miles off, and we soon became comparatively comfortable. But Rorke's Drift at best was a rat's-hole of a place, and though vigorous efforts were made to clear and cleanse the ground, there always seemed to be the smell of the dead Zulus in one's nostrils; and this was not imagination when the wind blew from the quarter towards which the line of Zulu retreat had lain.

For the first few days we were waiting hoping to hear of more survivors of Isandhlwana. We had heard of some having been seen fighting their way out of camp, and we hoped against hope they might have reached Helpmakaar, Utrecht, or some other point in safety; but none were heard of.

The only survivors who did reach Rorke's Drift *laager* were the dogs belonging to the camp, who kept coming back one by one, thin and poor, but seemingly overjoyed to get among the red-coats again. Most of them were cut with *assegais*. There were several terriers left in camp, but these apparently were not able to escape, or probably would not surrender and died with their masters.

Colonel Degacher, of the 2-24th, had left a well-bred pointer in camp, and for some days hoped the dog would find his way back to him. Days passed, and other dogs rejoined their corps, but Slap never put in an appearance. At length, at daybreak on the morning of the 5th of February, a fortnight after Isandhlwana, when the entrance to the *laager* was opened, there was the dog, having swum the river during the night, sitting on his haunches, waiting to be admitted. He was sadly cut by *assegais*, but seemed not to think about his wounds now that he had effected his escape.

CHAPTER 11

Maritzburg

At the end of the first week in February I left Rorke's Drift for Maritzburg to resume duties which the kindness of my chief had permitted me to lay aside for c while.

The country through which I passed was almost deserted; cottages, farmhouses, and in many places native *kraals*, all empty, and looking melancholy and forlorn. The white population had assembled together in *laager* for protection at the nearest magistracy or most defensible farmhouse, or had taken refuge in the towns and villages. In some cases the wayside inns, or "accommodation houses," were still open; but generally these also were shut up, and unless your food was on your saddle, you ran a good chance of having to tighten your belt and go supperless to sleep.

Two days and a half good riding brought me to Maritzburg. Preparations for the defence of the town were being pushed forward with all haste. The public buildings and portions of the streets which led from them, the gaol, and other strong places were being rendered more defensible. Business was in a great measure suspended, and the energies of every one were occupied in preparing to meet any Zulu inroad. The little town had quite lost its comfortable and homelike look. Anxious and care-worn faces were common in the streets; every other woman seemed to be in mourning, and almost every other man, if not in mourning, wore a slip of crape on his left arm *en militaire*, showing how many had been killed by the *assegai* of the Zulu warriors at Isandhlwana.

The danger of the situation was realized to the full, and the panic and excitement throughout the colony were very great, and the steamers from Natal to Cape Town carried many women and children out of the colony for safety.

If those writers who so freely expressed their opinions on the un-mixed benefits derived by Natal from the Zulu war, and who laid such stress on the large sums Natalians were supposed to be making, conse-quent on the outbreak of hostilities, had passed through the colony at this time, they would have thought, for people doing a thriving trade, that the colonists were somewhat depressed.

To say that Natal made direct profits out of the war is as just as to say that France made profit out of the German war, because there were scoundrels who sold paper boots and worthless rifles to Gam-betta's levies, or that England made profits out of the Ashantee war because a few gun-runners made their fortunes by selling the enemy bad guns and worse gunpowder,

A portion of the English press expected an outcry from the colony, on account of the sacrifices she was making and the losses in life and money she was suffering from the war, and being astonished that Na-tal, so far from making an outcry, was cheerfully and readily doing all her small white population could do to further the war, jumped at once to the conclusion—hardly a generous one—that she was mak-ing money out of it. The fact was that almost every white man in the colony, whether trader or farmer, knew that unless the Zulu power was broken, unless the menace of the Zulu army was done away with, the colony was not worth living in, and all made up their minds to undergo any sacrifice in order that their adopted land should become peaceful and secure.

What those sacrifices were it would have been well for English writers to understand before they wrote bitter words about English subjects far away.

It would have been well to realize how large a proportion of her male population Natal sent to fight side by side with the red-coats at the beginning of the Zulu war, and to understand that the mounted volunteers who did such good service were not men who went out against the Zulus from a wish for excitement or plunder, but were men who had no less worthy motive than that of literally fighting "for hearth and home."

Many of these men were married; almost all had either places of business which they were forced to close, or farms which they had to leave in charge of their native servants, chancing the loss of stock and movables.

People in England have never realized the gap in the colony made by the lives lost at Isandhlwana, nor understood how many families in Natal were sent into mourning by the losses among the colonial troops on that day.

And the accusation of some of the English, prints that Natal naturally did not object to the Zulu war, because she was seeing her battles fought for her and making money at the same time, was felt with a sense of injustice, the keenness of which needs a knowledge of colonists to understand.

The news of the Isandhlwana disaster caused a thrill of alarm or excitement throughout South Africa. Where the telegraph wire reached, the colonists first received the news; but where there was no telegraph, the natives first heard how the great king had now really begun to wash his *assegais*—how the English chief's camp had been taken, and the white soldiers eaten up by a Zulu *impi* as if they were only a handful—how the English had had to go back again into Natal; and there was not a petty chief or headman, though perhaps hundreds of miles from Zulu Land, who did not hold himself the higher on account of the prowess shown by the warriors of his own colour who were fighting on the banks of the Tugela and Buffalo.

The Zulu king lost no time in making known his victory. Messengers were sent off in all directions, hurrying with the brave news for the black man: to the north, to Sekukuni and the Boers; to the south, to the Amaponda and the Basutos; to the Gaikas and Galekas in the old colony—even, it is said, to the Korannas and Barolongs, and the Hottentot races bordering on the Kalahari desert, the same message went out.

This was immediately after the king received the news that the camp had been taken and the white men destroyed. He was told that the whole of the column had been eaten up, and that now there were only two English *impis* left to make away with. This was indeed good news, and worthy to be made known to all the black men in South Africa. But gradually Cetywayo learnt, not without difficulty, the whole truth.

The camp of the white men had been taken and much plunder, but not without great losses to the Zulu regiments. Most of them were so disorganized by fighting and plunder that they had dispersed to their *kraals*, and had not brought their booty to the king, according to his strict order. Moreover, only a part of the white soldiers were in the camp, and the other part of them had marched safely back into Natal.

Then the Englishman's column (General Pearson's) had beaten the *impi* sent against them, and had sat down at Ekowe, building a strong place there. Also that the Bagolusini Zulus could do nothing against the Dutchman's column (General Wood's); for the English *induna* who commanded there was very wary, and could not be surprised, and his horsemen were always harassing the Zulus in the neighbourhood.

The king also found out, after much inquiry, that the Tulwana had not sustained their losses at Isandhlwana, but had gone across the river and, commanded by Dabulamanzi, had attacked the house at the 'Tyshane (Rorke's Drift), and had been well beaten there. This made the Zulu king very angry, and he found that things were not going so well with him as it had appeared when the taking of the camp had been first reported to him.

In a few days, too, the news came to him that more red soldiers had come up out of the sea (detachments of the 4th and 88th Regiments, from the Cape Colony) to replace those eaten up at Isandhlwana. This looked bad. The old men round him shook their heads, took snuff, and said "*Waugh!*" (a Zulu exclamation which often means a great deal, and must be heard for its solemnity to be realized). "The white men, they had heard, could get as many men from the sea as they wished. Isandhlwana was all very well, but their young men had fallen like grass, and they were still dying like sick dogs in their *kraals* from their wounds; if the white men got men out of the sea to replace the men they (the Zulus) ate up, they would be able to go on fighting forever."

Altogether, the Zulu king thought it worth his while to see what a little diplomacy could now do; so he sent a message by a man of no position—who could be regarded as an official or an unofficial messenger, as seemed good hereafter—to say, "There had been some mistake. His troublesome young regiments had got him into a scrape again. The affair at Isandhlwana was entirely unintentional. The *impi* who had taken the English camp was only bringing the cattle to pay up the fine for Sirayo's sons, but the English had irritated some of his young regiments by firing at them, and they had attacked the white men in consequence. He was really much annoyed at the whole matter, and suggested that the English should retire back into Natal, and that they should talk the matter over in a friendly way."

★★★★★★

The news of Isandhlwana reached Maritzburg on the 24th of January, at eight in the morning, and the High Commissioner, in conjunction with the Lieutenant-Governor and the General commanding, took instant measures to meet the possible results of such a disaster, and to obtain such help as was to be found within reach, so as to strengthen to the utmost our position until reinforcements could arrive from England.

The departure of the steamer carrying the news of Isandhlwana and the demand for reinforcements was put forward twenty-four hours, which would just give her time to coal after her arrival in Table Bay from the eastern ports of the Cape Colony. She was ordered to leave her telegrams at St. Vincent, which was some five or six days nearer than Madeira.

A ship chancing to leave Durban for Mauritius, despatches were sent to the acting Governor of this island, the Hon. Napier Broome, informing him of the straits the neighbouring colony was in.

On receiving the news of Isandhlwana, the Cape Ministry promptly met in council, and decided (although the attitude of many of the native clans within its borders was causing considerable anxiety) to offer that every red-coat in the colony should be sent up to the front, and arranged to call out a regiment of yeomanry and various detachments of volunteers to take the place of the Imperial troops.

To us in England, who know how unwilling farmers are to leave their farms for any length of time, and how carefully the eight days for yeomanry training have to be chosen, so as not to interfere with any pressing farmer's work, it ought not to be hard to understand what a serious matter was the calling out suddenly, and for an indefinite period, a force composed of farmers in a purely agricultural country.

Nor ought it to be hard to understand the complications and difficulties which would ensue if a volunteer corps, raised, let us say, in Southampton, was called out for active service, and part of the corps sent, at a few days' notice, five or six hundred miles away—how the stores would lose storekeepers, the shops their shopmen, the banks their clerks, etc., etc.

There would be, however, one important difference—the places of the absentees could be readily filled from the immense labour supply ready to hand in the United Kingdom.

Be that as it may, one thing is certainly clear—that the English public has never understood or fully appreciated the way the Cape Colony gallantly and spontaneously came forward to the assistance of her sister colony; how readily she, at great cost and inconvenience to herself, called out her colonial troops, and so enabled every man of

Her Majesty's army to be sent to Natal.

I am aware that the history of the Zulu war has been graphically related by far abler pens than mine, but if this account of the commencement of it, from one on the spot at the time, is of any use in modifying the opinion held by many in England that the war was needlessly hurried on, I shall not feel that it has been written in vain.

LEONAUR

ALSO FROM LEONAUR

AVAILABLE IN SOFTCOVER OR HARDCOVER WITH DUST JACKET

THE 9TH—THE KING'S (LIVERPOOL REGIMENT) IN THE GREAT WAR 1914 - 1918 *by Enos H. G. Roberts*—Mersey to mud—war and Liverpool men.

THE GAMBARDIER *by Mark Severn*—The experiences of a battery of Heavy artillery on the Western Front during the First World War.

FROM MESSINES TO THIRD YPRES *by Thomas Floyd*—A personal account of the First World War on the Western front by a 2/5th Lancashire Fusilier.

THE IRISH GUARDS IN THE GREAT WAR - VOLUME 1 *by Rudyard Kipling*—Edited and Compiled from Their Diaries and Papers—The First Battalion.

THE IRISH GUARDS IN THE GREAT WAR - VOLUME 1 *by Rudyard Kipling*—Edited and Compiled from Their Diaries and Papers—The Second Battalion.

ARMOURED CARS IN EDEN *by K. Roosevelt*—An American President's son serving in Rolls Royce armoured cars with the British in Mesopatamia & with the American Artillery in France during the First World War.

CHASSEUR OF 1914 *by Marcel Dupont*—Experiences of the twilight of the French Light Cavalry by a young officer during the early battles of the great war in Europe.

TROOP HORSE & TRENCH *by R.A. Lloyd*—The experiences of a British Lifeguardsman of the household cavalry fighting on the western front during the First World War 1914-18.

THE EAST AFRICAN MOUNTED RIFLES *by C.J. Wilson*—Experiences of the campaign in the East African bush during the First World War.

THE LONG PATROL *by George Berrie*—A Novel of Light Horsemen from Gallipoli to the Palestine campaign of the First World War.

THE FIGHTING CAMELIERS *by Frank Reid*—The exploits of the Imperial Camel Corps in the desert and Palestine campaigns of the First World War.

STEEL CHARIOTS IN THE DESERT *by S. C. Rolls*—The first world war experiences of a Rolls Royce armoured car driver with the Duke of Westminster in Libya and in Arabia with T.E. Lawrence.

WITH THE IMPERIAL CAMEL CORPS IN THE GREAT WAR *by Geoffrey Inchbald*—The story of a serving officer with the British 2nd battalion against the Senussi and during the Palestine campaign.

www.ingramcontent.com/pod-product-compliance
Lightning Source LLC
Chambersburg PA
CBHW031901090426
42741CB00005B/596